THE REFERENCE SHELF

Vol. 27

No. 2

OUR NATURAL RESOURCES
THEIR DEVELOPMENT AND USE

Edited by
JUANITA MORRIS KREPS

THE H. W. WILSON COMPANY
NEW YORK   1955

PREFACE

After successive years of thinking about unemployment, reemployment, full employment, about factory production, inflation and deflation, and hundreds of other matters in the structure of economic life, the United States must now give new and deep consideration to the fundamental upon which all employment, all daily activity, eventually rests: the contents of the earth and its physical environment.—*Report of the President's Materials Policy Commission. June 1952. Volume I, page 1.*

As the above quotation indicates, the postwar years have witnessed a revival of national interest in our natural resources, their conservation and control. This renewed concern over our nation's "resource base" grows in part out of our World War II experience with the rapid rate of resource depletion brought about by total war. In part also, it stems from the knowledge that our postwar economy, with its complex technology and high levels of output, has utilized and will continue to utilize resources at a rate far higher than that of our prewar experience.

It has become increasingly clear that the public interest requires action in all reasonable ways to conserve our resources—especially the energy resources, and the life-sustaining resources, such as water—as well as increased efficiency in the use of those resources, and advanced technology in the use of "substitute" resources, such as atomic energy, which are just now becoming available. There is no disagreement about this general proposition. The debates, often acrimonious, and the discussions, frequently heated, on natural resource policy are almost always concerned with the answer to one basic question: To what extent should private property and enterprise yield to public policy? That is, to what extent should the conservation and control of our existing resources, and the development of new resources, be left in private hands, and to what extent should these tasks be assumed by government?

This is obviously not a purely economic question. In fact, political overtones obscure the basic economic issues as often as not. But it is just as obviously a very important question from the standpoint of the national interest, and the answer that is finally evolved will have considerable effect on our future national well being. Consequently, the issue of private versus public ownership and control of our natural resources seems very much worth studying.

Historically, the Democratic party has favored more public control of resources and the Republican party more private control. Hence it was only natural to expect some changes in our national policy on natural resources, which had been developed and administered along Democratic lines since 1933, when the Republicans succeeded to power in 1953. The changes have come, or have been recommended as Administration policy. They have provoked bitter, partisan debate as well as thoughtful discussion. And they have created "issues" that have raised again the questions of who shall conserve and control, and to what extent, in several resource areas—the "tidelands" (oil), other public lands (timber, grazing rights, subsurface mineral rights), and hydroelectric power ("Dixon-Yates" and Hell's Canyon). The pros and cons of these issues are covered in the second, third, and fourth sections of this volume, following an introductory section on background and principles of national resource policy that aims at giving the reader the necessary minimum of perspective needed to grapple with the discussions of specific issues.

The fifth section deals with our newest resource, atomic energy, and with the question of who shall develop its tremendous potential as an energy source. Here national policy is still tentative and unsettled. On the one hand, security considerations and the tremendous investment that the American people, through their government, have made in atomic processes point toward continued public development and control of the industry. On the other, the fact that the public investment in atomic energy was impelled by war and defense necessities, the great promise of the atom as a peacetime power source, and the American tradition of private initiative and enterprise, all favor atomic development by private industry. In such a mixed situation, "solution by compromise" is almost sure to result, under which there will be, in some degree, both public and private participation in the control and development of the applications of nuclear fission to peacetime, as well as military uses. And this, too, is in keeping with American tradition.

The editor gratefully acknowledges the copyright permissions and other courtesies that have facilitated the completion of her work.

JUANITA MORRIS KREPS

March 1, 1955

CONTENTS

I. OWNERSHIP AND CONTROL OF OUR NATURAL RESOURCES: BACKGROUND AND PRINCIPLES

EDITOR'S INTRODUCTION

Although tidelands oil was one of the big issues of the 1952 elections, and hydroelectric power similarly significant in the fall of 1954, the ownership and control of other natural resources is also at issue at the present time. The Eisenhower Administration has spoken of a "partnership" arrangement between government and private industry, and deplored signs of "creeping socialism," while critics have described the Administration's policy as a "giveaway," maintaining that only private industry stands to gain by Republican proposals relating to tidelands oil, the public lands, control of atomic energy, and electric power.

The background of the controversy over the control of our natural resources is developed below. In the first article, Mr. Stead poses the issue and lists major arguments set forth by the proponents of government ownership and regulation, and those in defense of private management. Professor Zimmermann then analyzes the political philosophy which led to the renewed interest in natural resources during the New Deal period, and to an increased Federal participation in resource management.

During the Truman Administration the major governmental survey of natural resources was the report of the President's Materials Policy Commission, popularly known as the Paley Commission Report. The third article, outlining the Commission's fundamental beliefs regarding the role of the Federal Government in insuring adequate future resources, is followed by a strong criticism of the Commission's point of view.

In contrast to the New Deal and the Truman policies on natural resources, Secretary of the Interior Douglas McKay discusses the economic and political philosophy characterizing the Republican Administration, which is attempting to "take America back from the bureaucrats and return it to the citizens of the nation." Criticism of these steps is offered in "The Great Giveaway," estimating that $100 billion has been given to private interests in the Administration's first two years; and support of the Administration's actions follows in "Give Away What?" which defends the tidelands oil decision, the revision of the 1946 Atomic Energy Act, and the current hydroelectric power policy.

THE ISSUE OF OWNERSHIP AND CONTROL OF NATURAL RESOURCES [1]

One of the major issues in economic policy relates to the ownership and control of natural resources and their products.

Should the basic natural resources, such as forests and grazing land, mineral-bearing lands, water supplies, and hydroelectric power sites, be owned and developed exclusively by private management under the free enterprise system, or should there be government ownership or regulation of these resources and activities?

Should the marketing and processing of these materials and energy sources be under private or public control?

The arguments on both sides of these issues are many and are put forward with vigor by their proponents.

In some free world countries the Socialist viewpoint predominates, holding that these great natural resources should be primarily under government management and control. We are not talking about communism or totalitarian dictatorship here, merely pointing out that some nations hold

[1] From *Economic Problems of Natural Resources,* pamphlet by William H. Stead, economist and resource management consultant. Joint Council on Economic Education. 2 West 46th Street. New York 36. 1955. Reprinted by permission.

to a different economic view of the proper management of resources, for example Sweden and Great Britain.

Other nations, like the United States, hold that to the maximum degree possible, private enterprise should develop the resources, subject to necessary governmental intervention and controls to protect the present and future welfare of the nation. . . .

Those who favor leaving these economic activities almost entirely to private enterprise, with little or no government intervention, are described by their opponents as "selfish economic reactionaries," while those who favor substantial participation by government are labeled "New Deal Socialists" by their opponents.

Leaving out the campaign oratory, it can be said that the Democratic party supports an economic policy favoring a larger share of government responsibility for the control and development of our natural resources, and the Republican party favors a policy of restricting such government intervention and doing as much of the job as possible under private auspices.

The fact that roughly half the people concerned with these issues hold to each of these positions indicates that there are sound arguments on both sides, and it is a question of balance and degree of emphasis.

Let us take a few examples of natural resources and see how these questions arise.

The forest resources include the trees, fish and wildlife, grazing lands, vegetative cover to retain rainfall and wilderness and scenic values.

During the early history of this nation these resources seemed limitless and the problem was how to harvest the products and make them available to meet people's demands.

We believed, and correctly, that the private ownership and management system, sparked by the profit motive, would get these products out faster and more efficiently than government management would.

Consequently there were no government controls or restrictions on this activity. In fact the government gave title to forest lands to those who wanted to develop the products and encouraged private enterprise by granting forest lands to railroads if they would build railroads to help the private owners get out their logs, lumber, and other products, and to mining companies that wanted to secure the minerals under the forest lands.

What was the result? We developed great industries based on forest products serving a host of human wants and needs. But, the private profit management system offered no adequate long run incentive to use the forest resources wisely and manage these great renewable resources so they would replenish themselves. The result we all know. We cut off most of our virgin timber; we destroyed or decimated some species of wildlife (buffalo for example); we removed the protective vegetative cover and created floods, draining off water supplies and eroding the soils and grazing lands.

Finally, as a nation we awoke to the danger of destroying these resources and under the leadership of Theodore Roosevelt, Gifford Pinchot, and others we passed laws which limited private management and put the government into the forest management business in several ways.

We set aside large acreages as national forests to be managed by the United States Forest Service. Many states likewise created state-owned forests. Here even the selective cutting of trees and the arrangements for grazing on forest lands are government controlled, although the logs are sold to private business and the grazing livestock are privately owned.

To protect fish and wildlife we passed laws regulating hunting and fishing and the government undertook to maintain fish hatcheries and wildlife refuges.

To preserve the wilderness and scenic values of forest areas, we created national parks and state parks and maintain them at government expense for the enjoyment of the people.

Although much of this government activity in forest management is now generally accepted as necessary if we are to preserve these renewable resources, some people feel the government intervention has gone too far. Thus bills have been introduced in . . . Congress to return some national forests and even national park lands to private control. Other proposals would weaken the government controls over grazing and mineral development on the forest lands in favor of the livestock raisers and the mining companies.

How our forest resources should be controlled and managed is thus still a very live economic issue.

What we have said about the forest resources applies in large part to the other natural resources. We now have a mixture of government and private management in the control and development of all these resources.

In some cases private enterprise predominates. For example, agricultural lands are almost entirely privately owned and managed. Even here, however, government does much of the research in production methods (through agricultural extension divisions and experiment stations) and it exercises important controls in the marketing activities (grading meat and food products, fixing "price floors," and regulating commodity exchanges, for example).

In other cases, government management and control of the natural resources predominates. Thus the navigable waters of our streams, rivers and lakes are under government control, even including the hydroelectric power sites. The power sites may be leased to private companies to develop and navigation rights may be granted to private transportation companies, or these activities may also be carried on by government.

The mineral resources fall somewhere in between. Some of the mineral-bearing lands are government owned and controlled as in many western states, and in the offshore submerged lands (recently involved in the tidelands oil controversy) ; others are privately owned.

Most of the economic activities related to securing the mineral products are privately owned and managed, from mining and well drilling through marketing, manufacturing, and selling the products.

However, the government closely regulates these private activities through commissions controlling the mining and well drilling leases, the freight rates and transportation charges, franchises for distributing gas and electricity, qualities of drugs and other products, and rates and prices in many instances. The government also exercises foreign trade controls and levies taxes, some of which are designed either to encourage or slow down the mining or development of a particular resource.

It has been indicated that a chief reason for the government's participation in the management and development of natural resources is to prevent unwise exploitation of an exhaustible or renewable resource.

In addition to this consideration, two other factors have led to government controls. One is to prevent private monopoly and resulting high prices. Particularly the energy resources are subject to monopoly control. For example, a hydroelectric power site can only be efficiently developed by one producer who then might be in a position to charge "monopoly prices" or rates. Similarly where the sources of a mineral are very limited, as in nickel or petroleum, monopoly control can result. Also the *distribution* of energy supplies, such as electricity and gas, tends toward monopoly since competing transmission lines or gas mains are wasteful.

This situation leads to government regulation, or government ownership and management, to protect the consumer. These regulations include distribution franchises, rate and quality controls, antitrust legislation, etc.

The other consideration leading to government regulation and control is to protect the health and safety of the public from harmful materials and products and against dangerous processes. The food and drug acts, and safety inspection and regulation of factories, transportation facilities and public utilities are illustrations.

There are scores of small issues included in this larger one of public vs. private management and control of our natural resources. In all of them it is a question of degree. We all agree that if we are to *conserve* and *develop* our natural resources *wisely*, it must be a joint effort of government and private enterprise. We differ honestly on the relative emphasis, but one thing is clear whether we like it or not—the government's share of this joint responsibility is far larger in the 1950's than it was in the 1850's!

THE NEW DEAL AND THE NEW ASSET CONSCIOUSNESS [2]

The most powerful blow struck in defense of . . . [natural resources] has come . . . not from technology, not from changing costs, but from changes in human attitudes, attitudes which imperceptibly emerge from the womb of social philosophy and take on tangible form in rewritten and reinterpreted laws and in revised public policies. In the United States these new attitudes with their tangible aftermath are largely identified with the New Deal. But that is not quite accurate. The roots of the new movement, the origin of the new way of viewing our natural and national endowment of basic assets, reach further back in time, to the conservationists of Theodore Roosevelt's day. One of the greatest of the new hydroelectric enterprises—the Boulder Canyon Project, the keystone of which is the Hoover Dam—was started under President Hoover, years before the phrase "the New Deal" was coined.

The crux of the new philosophy is the realization that, in the long run, the magnificent achievements made under private capitalistic enterprise are endangered by inadequate regard for the durable basic assets, natural and cultural, on which all economic life depends, and for the conditions, forces, and processes of nature which underlie all human endeavor. So-called laws of short-range profit-seeking market economics come into progressively serious conflicts with the laws of nature. A young continent can stand a great deal of punishment from men unaware of the mysteries of

[2] From *World Resources and Industries* (revised edition), by Erich W. Zimmermann, distinguished professor of resources, University of Texas. Harper & Bros. New York. 1951. p571-5. Reprinted by permission.

ecology. But inevitably the time comes when man must take account of the situation, call a halt to his destructive folly, and make his peace with nature. Few people not ideologically warped in their judgment will seriously question the glorious achievements of the free enterprise system which have helped to make the United States the richest, freest, most powerful country in the world. But one would have to be blind not to see the terrific cost in impaired basic assets—eroded soil, polluted rivers, gutted forests, overgrazed ranges, and, last but not least, blighted or frustrated humanity—at which this progress was bought. . . .

The collapse of the boom in 1929 and the Great Depression that followed shook people's faith to its foundations—faith in the bonanza of untrammeled private enterprise and undiluted laissez faire. A reaction was inevitable. The pendulum had to swing back. Men searched for the deeper meaning of economics and inevitably came face to face with ecology. Those who had long been market-conscious at last became resource-conscious.

In the ecological scheme of things water plays a vital part. If properly cared for, water is the bringer of life; if neglected, it can be the cause of disaster. And it has been neglected by the market-conscious leaders of our economy. Every year water-induced erosion ruins large amounts of topsoil. Every year floods destroy vast property values and take an intolerable toll of human life. Rivers are polluted with the sewage of a thousand cities. Wild life is suffering. Human health is endangered. Rivers are silting up and blocking navigation.

Here was a vast field in which governments—local, state, and Federal—could perform prodigious feats without stepping on the toes of private business. If government had not done this long before, it was due partly to incomplete realization on the part of both experts and laymen of this vital necessity, partly to the failure of penny-wise and pound-foolish congressmen to appropriate the necessary funds. But now all this changed. Business was unable—in the Depression—to take care of the livelihood of large portions of the population. The government had to step in. Here was the golden opportunity to make up for decades, perhaps a century, of neglect. Many of the "alphabet agencies" such as CCC [Civilian Conservation Corps] and PWA [Public Works Administration] helped to tackle the new task of saving and improving our basic assets, especially soil and water. . . .

The government entered the field of electric power generation on a vast scale. That this step, which was merely incidental in a far vaster scheme of watershed control and regional resources development, was fought savagely by private utilities goes without saying. During its first years the TVA [Tennessee Valley Authority] was engaged in a continuous struggle in the courts, the lower courts generally siding with the private power companies, and the Supreme Court with the government. The crux of the issue was whether society could afford to forego the enormous by-product benefits of vast amounts of electric energy that were generated in connection with the performance of legitimate government functions, simply because certain conflicts with private business interests were inevitable.

The struggle was sharpened by a number of circumstances associated with the economic and political atmosphere of the period—the early years of the New Deal and the Roosevelt Administration, and the Great Depression. It was a time when, because of the business depression, demand for electricity was at a low point. At the same time the Federal Trade Commission was carrying on its investigation of the power industry (resulting in a monumental report of eighty-four volumes). This, in turn, led to strong legislative measures designed to stop the abuses revealed in the report. Particularly prominent in this reform movement were the Public Utilities Act of 1935 . . . and the act establishing the Securities and Exchange Commission. Feelings ran high. The cry of "economic royalists" was heard. . . . It was not the ideal climate in which to begin a social experiment of unprecedented boldness.

In particular the problem of rates charged for electric power generated much heat. Under regulation by state public service commissions, private power companies had been able, by and large, to do just about as they pleased. The laws governing the valuation of properties, on which the whole structure of rate regulation was based, were extremely lax; the investor was usually favored, the consumer seldom. Now the Federal Power Commission was entrusted with the task of probing into the valuation of all power companies engaged in interstate commerce. . . .

A fundamental philosophy of pricing is involved which cannot be brushed aside. Those responsible for TVA felt, or rather concluded from the evidence before them, that the private power industry was caught in a vicious circle of high rates, low consumption, and high costs. Private companies, in general, tend to be timid about reducing rates, knowing that once this has been done, perhaps experimentally, it is politically impossible to raise them again, for regulating commissions would not dare to face the uproar of public indignation. Some companies did experiment with "objective rates" and "promotional rates." But, with rare exceptions, they refused to "gamble" on the stimulating effect of low rates on use. TVA, on the other hand, perhaps influenced by Ford's magnificent success with his low-priced mass-produced mass-consumed car and impressed by the fact that electric power is one of the great blessings of mankind, struck out boldly with rates so low that consumption responded almost immediately. And just as surely as mass consumption of Ford cars made possible their mass production, and just as surely as mass production lowered unit cost and price and thus stimulated mass consumption, so that fortunate nexus between larger use, larger output, and low unit cost is equally operative in the case of electricity. The responsiveness of demand to lowered rates was skillfully prodded by energetic sales campaigns offering appliances at reduced prices.

Low rates for electricity attract industries, electrical machinery raises the productivity of labor, this in turn raises incomes and the standard of living, and this again calls for the use of more electricity. Similarly on the farm, the liberal use of electricity renders labor more productive and sets in motion a spiral of forces which raises the whole level of the economy. A successful farmer takes care of his farm—he stops erosion, which in turn reduces run-off, which eases the task of flood control.

Thus TVA initiated what may be called an A-to-Z approach to the problem of regional development. Whether the success of the experiment had anything to do with the fact that private utilities later entered the rural areas with as much gusto as they had previously shunned them is a moot question. In recent years the private power industry has added millions of farmers to its lists of customers and has not lost money in doing so. The enormous improvement in the American farmer's economic status that resulted from the fantastically high prices for agricultural products undoubtedly had much to do with opening up rural America as a profitable field for the sale of electricity.

When the Roosevelt Administration pushed the development of publicly controlled hydroelectricity in different sections of the country, first in the Tennessee Valley—the Hoover Dam had been started under the Republican Administration—then in the Northwest (especially Bonneville and Grand Coulee), the Mississippi valley, California, and elsewhere, there went up a hue and cry against the "insane" enlargement of the nation's power supply beyond reasonable limits and the generation of power in parts of the country that seemed to offer no possible power market even in the future. The government was accused of the reckless spending of public funds. The Administration, however, apparently took the position that there cannot be an oversupply of as vital a commodity as electrical energy, there can only be underconsumption. And sufficient rate inducements can create the demand.

FUNDAMENTAL CONCEPTS OF NATIONAL
RESOURCE POLICY [3]

We believe in private enterprise as the most efficacious way of performing industrial tasks in the United States. With this belief, a belief in the spur of the profit motive and what is called "the price system" obviously goes hand in hand. This method, motive, and system have served uniquely well in America. They have brought us to a commanding industrial position, promoting growth and keeping the basic costs of production low so that the standard of living could reach its present high levels. We believe in a minimum of interference with these patterns of private enterprise. But to believe in a minimum of interference is not to believe that this minimum must be set at zero. Private enterprise itself has from time to time asked for helps, or restraints, or counterpoises from government to keep the system working at its best; for this reason, among others, we have experienced for a long time a mixture of private and public influences on the functioning of our economy. The Commission sees no reason either to blink this fact or to decry it; as we see the future, the co-existence of great private and public strength is not only desirable but essential to our preservation. . . .

It is the Commission's belief that the bulk of the task of insuring adequate future materials supply can best be carried out by private business under the competitive market structure, operating within broad policy outlines which it is the responsibility of government to provide.

In the United States, the free price system has always been the great "allocator" of resources and materials. It provides a combination of incentives and discouragements to which private business and consumers variously respond in making investments, raising or lowering production, directing technological efforts, substituting materials, and so on. This

[3] From *Foundations for Growth and Security*, vol 1 of *Resources for Freedom; a Report to the President*, by the President's Materials Policy Commission (better known as the Paley Commission, after its chairman, William F. Paley). Supt. of Docs. Washington 25, D.C. 1952. p3, 17-20.

system in effect spreads decision making over millions of people and provides a strong incentive to efficiency. On the whole, it produces good results when judged by its service to the public interests—but not always perfect results. A brief hypothetical case may serve to illustrate the system's relationship to the domain of materials, and to distinguish the roles of private enterprise and government.

As production of a material, say copper, begins to press on its resource base—that is, as demand for it grows while further expansion is no longer profitable at current prices from known resources—its price rises. This rise of price is the signal to producers to turn out more, to consumers to look for substitutes. Both signals are heeded. The first stimulates production at home, and imports from abroad. If the price continues high, there is encouragement to new discoveries and for better technology to bring lower grade materials into production. The second signal makes it profitable now to use other materials where copper was used before. Engineers ponder how to achieve the performance they want using something cheaper than copper. If, meanwhile, some improvements are made in the technique of producing such a substitute as aluminum, further substitutions may lessen demand for copper and take some pressure off the price. Thus copper may end up only moderately higher in price, but used only for those particular needs that make a higher price acceptable. In a growing economy, the absolute amount of copper used may not decline under these hypothetical circumstances, but its percentage of the expanding total materials stream will shrink.

For many reasons the actual course of events is unlikely to be so smooth. Increasing prices may fail to bring out as much production as would be profitable at that price. Mine operators may not expect the price to stay high; investment conditions, or attitudes of this or foreign governments, may impede production or slow export expansion. Inventors may turn too late to devising better methods, or long years may elapse between the development of better techniques and their actual adoption. Research that would benefit all may not repay any one enterprise. And depressions, in the past, have demonstrated that the price system cannot handle all problems.

There is accordingly room for an economic materials policy. The guide to public action must therefore be a study of where the private market works so imperfectly that something must be done about it.

The Federal Government carries out many materials programs costing hundreds of millions of dollars and involving dozens of agencies. The Federal Government has six major roles:

As conditioner of the economic environment, the government, through tax policies, fiscal, monetary, and credit policies, labor policies, and the enforcement of the antitrust laws, affects private costs, prices and profits, and hence in many cases influences materials production and use.

As regulator of private industry, in the protection of the public interest, the government affects the rates and markets of "natural monopolies" in the fields of electric power and natural gas. The allocation of scarce materials and the curtailment of their use under emergency conditions provide other examples of regulation.

As guardian of foreign relations and national security, the government has in recent years greatly expanded its activities in the materials field. Where security needs require developing resources more swiftly and producing materials in greater volume than provided by ordinary market incentives, government uses such devices as market guarantees, development grants and loans, long-term purchase contracts, and rapid tax amortization. With friendly nations abroad it participates in emergency international materials allocation programs. It plays a large role in establishing the framework within which private companies of the United States do business abroad. Through the Export-Import Bank, [the] Point Four [program], the use of foreign aid counterpart funds, and as a member of the International Bank for Reconstruction and Development, the government provides encouragement to foreign resource development. The general import and export of materials is subject to direct government regulation by tariffs and export controls.

As owner and custodian of resources, the government is the landlord of vast areas of mineral lands, proved and potential; of forest and grazing lands, and supervisor of all navigable rivers and streams and coastal waters. Its rules governing the use of publicly owned resources vary in the extreme.

As supplier of services to private industry, the government supports the mapping work of the United States Geological Survey and many activities of the Bureau of Mines, including its technical research and development work on such problems as manganese and shale oil, and its statistical publications, designed to help private industry. In the Department of Agriculture, programs of technical research and educational service, soil conservation, and pest control are designed to strengthen the economic position of producers and the resources with which they work. Programs to curb forest fires, diseases, and pests, are calculated to strengthen the long-range supply of forest products to private producers.

As buyer and user of materials, the Federal Government is a major purchaser and user of materials in the United States economy, its military, foreign aid, and construction programs accounting for the bulk of what it buys. It thus exerts strong influence on market conditions, as in stockpile buying. Through its research and testing activities it greatly affects product development, design, standards, and specifications. The efficiency with which government itself uses materials has a heavy bearing upon the whole materials situation.

Local governments and especially state governments are also deeply involved in the resource and materials field: the control of utility rates and of water pollution; the regulation of oil and gas production in the name of conservation; the regulation of timber cutting practices; the ownership of forest and other resource-bearing lands; the taxing of resources, and the large-scale purchase and use of materials are examples.

These various activities of the Federal, state, and local governments form an extensive and complex pattern. It is not surprising that the elements of the pattern are sometimes inconsistent and badly out of balance when measured against the ideal of a comprehensive and unified national materials policy. In a strict sens', this pattern of governmental materials policies and programs is not a pattern at all, but a loose array of measures which influence the nation's present and prospective materials position.

THE PALEY REPORT AND PRIVATE ENTERPRISE [4]

Some of the recommendations made by the Commission are based on a political and economic philosophy which, if put into practice, would serve to undermine our present system of private enterprise.

Let me illustrate what I mean. When I began reading the Paley Commission Report I was greatly impressed by what appeared to be the Commission's credo. On page 3 of volume I, I came across this very significant statement:

We believe in private enterprise as the most efficacious way of performing industrial tasks in the United States. With this belief, a belief in the spur of the profit motive and what is called 'the price system' obviously goes hand in hand. This method, motive, and system have served uniquely well in America.

And listen to this sentence, which is still a part of the quote:

We believe in a minimum of interference with these patterns of private enterprise.

Bearing in mind that this sound principle came from a Commission that had been appointed by an Administration

[4] From remarks of Joseph Zimmerman, editor-in-chief, *Daily Metal Reporter.* In *Resources: From Abundance to Scarcity by 1975?* Text of a round table discussion, sponsored by the National Industrial Conference Board, of the report of the President's Materials Policy Commission (Paley Commission). (Studies in Business Economics no36) The Board. 247 Park Avenue. New York 17. 1952. p 19-24. Reprinted by permission.

whose political and economic philosophy is based on New Dealism and Fair Dealism, I could not help but think of that famous line in Shakespeare's *Merchant of Venice*: "A Daniel has come to judgment."

However, this feeling of satisfaction and approval did not last very long. . . .

Private enterprise, the profit motive, the price system are all good in the Commission's opinion—but, says the Commission . . .:

To believe in a minimum of interference is not to believe that the minimum must be set at zero.

When you read this statement you ask yourself: How much above zero does the Commission want the government to interfere with business? As I read the Commission's recommendations I was shocked by the degree, or by the number of degrees above zero, that the Commission favors government interference. . . .

I began to wonder, as I read the Report, whether our capitalistic system, and our private enterprise system, which made this country the greatest in the world, supplying our civilian requirements in times of peace and becoming the arsenal for the democracies of the world in times of war—whether this private enterprise system had outlived its usefulness, whether it had become so decrepit, so outmoded, and so old that it required government crutches to support it.

This is no idle flight of the imagination. Let me quote you the Commission's own words:

It is the Commission's belief that the bulk of the task of insuring adequate future supply can best be carried out by private business under the competitive market structure, operating within the broad policy outlines which it is the responsibility of government to provide.

In other words, the government is to call the tunes and business is to dance to them.

The Commission admits that some government activities, or what I would term government meddling with business, have been inconsistent and badly coordinated, such as market

guarantees, government loans, long-term purchasing contracts, international allocations, utilization of counterpart
funds, stockpiling, etc., etc. But the Commission believes
that these activities can be improved upon. . . .

You ask yourself: who are the supermen in our government who are so superbly equipped through training and
experience to be able to tell the metal-mining industry how
to conduct its business, or how to market its commodities?

It is because the metal-mining industry has been a private
enterprise and has functioned under private management that
it has achieved a stage of development second to none in the
world. Therein lies the danger of the Paley Commission's
philosophy and its recommendations; namely, that anything
that private industry can do, the government can do better.

Nor can I agree with the Commission when it takes as
one of its main tenets that "it is the function of the government to reduce market instability." The Commission makes
a great to-do about the market instability in metals.

I was brought up in the old school that it was the law
of supply and demand, rather than government laws, that
determined market trends. As a matter of fact, events have
proved that every time the government has interfered with
the law of supply and demand, we have had greater market
instability; and, of course, the taxpayers have had to carry
the burden. . . .

For example, the Paley Commission favors the International Materials Conference plan, which seeks to limit, by
means of international allocations, the amount of copper and
nickel and zinc, and other metals, that we in this country
may consume. We have had a taste of the effects of this
plan on domestic industry.

Let me give you a concrete illustration as to what happens when our government, in cooperation with other foreign governments, tells private industry how much copper
or other metals may be consumed. The Scovill Manufacturing Company, of Waterbury, Connecticut, is the world's
largest producer of steel and brass safety pins. The com-

pany produces hundreds of other items, but with respect to safety pins it stands first in the world. The government prohibited the company from making the kind of safety pins it always made because the raw materials that the company needed were going abroad. The company's foreign competitors, however, were able to produce the pins that Scovill's customers wanted; and today these foreign competitors enjoy about 25 per cent of the total market in the United States, and Scovill can't do a thing about it.

Now multiply this situation a hundredfold, or a thousandfold, and we get an idea of what is likely to happen to American private industry if we were to follow the Commission's suggestion that "the United States should take the initiative in urging more vigorous international action to solve trade and distribution problems that can be dealt with effectively only on an international basis."

As a means of reducing market instability, the Paley Commission favors the creation of buffer stocks of metal. It favors the creation of an international agency to manage the buffer pool; and this agency would have the power to decide what metals to buy, when to accumulate, and when to sell. The governments would own these metals and could dump them on the markets when they saw fit. Uncle Sam, of course, would have to bear the cost of the plan.

The international agency would also have the power to impose quotas on production, sales, and imports as a means of eliminating sharp market fluctuations. If that is not market manipulation of the worst kind, I don't know what is. We have had such buffer pools in the past. Private industry tried them and they failed, because they interfered with the natural functioning of the law of supply and demand.

The Paley Commission, however, is convinced that its own buffer pool, along with its quotas and limitations on use, would not fail simply because it would be inaugurated by governments and would be controlled by governments. In other words, where you have a government cartel, or a government commodity agreement, or government market manipulations, they are good, *per se*, simply because they constitute legalized meddling with the law of supply and demand, and with private enterprise.

In spite of the many protestations by the Paley Commission that it is in favor of our private enterprise system, as I read the Commission's report I got the distinct impression it believed that the private enterprise system can only function successfully under government meddling, which the Commission calls government control or supervision.

We are now reaping the benefits of such government meddling in the domestic copper market. Those of you who are in the metal business know the situation that now prevails with respect to the price of copper. Copper of domestic origin may only sell for 24½ cents a pound, while copper of foreign origin may and does sell at 36½ cents a pound. . . .

Even if the social planners could guarantee us the market stability that is envisioned by the Paley Commission, I doubt whether it would be worth the price we would have to pay. I am very much afraid that the cure recommended by the Commission to eliminate the evils which it believes are inherent in the private enterprise system might kill the patient.

GAINS IN RESOURCES CONTROL [5]

President Eisenhower has said one of the prime purposes of his Administration is to take America back from the bureaucrats and return it to the citizens of the nation. That is a thumbnail summary of what we have been trying to do in the Department of the Interior—bring closer to the people most directly concerned the many important activities of the Federal Government in managing the nation's natural resources.

When I became Secretary of the Interior in January 1953, I found bureaucratic concentration of resource management responsibility approaching the danger point. Es-

[5] From report by Douglas McKay, Secretary of the Interior (one of a series of mid-term reports prepared by members of the Administration at the request of the New York *Herald Tribune*). New York *Herald Tribune.* p 1+. October 22, 1954. Reprinted by permission.

sential development work was slowing down because of endless red tape. Decisions based on doctrinaire ideologies, rather than on grass-roots understanding of the national resource problems, were creating a veritable hodgepodge.

Most important of all, of course, by depriving local people of any responsibility for resource management, the government was losing the broad base of support for resource conservation. Such support, in my opinion, spells the difference between a successful long-range program and a hit-or-miss program of expediency.

We decided to do something about it.

The first major fact we faced was that the Department of the Interior is composed of eleven separate bureaus and services having many diverse interests. The underlying common denominator of the activities of all of these bureaus is natural resources, but their specific functions range from water and power, public lands and minerals to fish and wildlife, national parks and Indian affairs. In many respects, these bureaus tended to go their own ways without adequate coordination of their activities.

To assure the necessary coordination in moving toward the common goal of resource development in the interest of all the people, the secretarial office was strengthened. Legal services were consolidated. Assistant secretaries were assigned specific responsibilities for direction of various bureaus.

Finally, all of the individual bureaus and services were carefully analyzed by groups of eminent citizens drawn from the professions, educational institutions, business conservation interests and other levels of government.

The independent decisions resulting from these surveys confirmed our initial judgment that decentralization of the activities of the department was necessary to bring it closer to its working areas.

The majority of the reorganization recommendations have been approved. Many of the necessary changes have been completed or are in the process of completion. Results so far indicate that we are succeeding in bringing the management of natural resources close to the people—where it belongs. . . .

Similar approaches, adapted to the problems that may be faced, are being developed in all of the resource areas for which the department is responsible. The basic theme has been to work in cooperation, wherever possible, with the state and local groups who know their own problems best and who, when approached with the friendly hand of partnership rather than the bureaucratic edict, are ready to pitch in and help.

We have found this to be the case in the dramatic new local interest in power development which has its inspiration from the President's partnership power program.

In the Pacific Northwest the new teamwork policy has given impetus to both public and privately owned utilities in accelerating power development to meet urgent power requirements. Non-Federal utilities now have thirty-three power projects, with a potential capacity of about 5.4 million kilowatts, under active consideration in the region. . . .

The fundamental difference between our policy and that of previous Administrations has been to get away from the concept that only the Federal Government has the wisdom, the know-how and the money to do the job. We believe that the job of supplying the power needs is so great that it requires the united efforts of all—Federal, state or local.

The task of resource conservation and development is a never-ending one, of course. But we believe that by basing the department's policies on a realistic program of grass-roots cooperation, we are laying the cornerstone for the type of resource progress that America needs.

THE GREAT GIVEAWAY [6]

Back in February 1953, when the first trainloads of eager lobbyists began pouring into Washington to greet the new

[6] From editorial. *Nation.* 179:269-72. October 2, 1954. Reprinted by permission.

Administration, Bruce Catton, our correspondent there, took one look and reported:

> They are coming in hungry, and they are not hungry for peanuts. The vast public-utility, oil, mining, and lumber interests that supported the Republican campaign are getting ready to move in on America's natural resources, and what they want is all the country has got. The new Administration is prepared to make things easy for them, and the program is beginning to look clear. It adds up to what is probably the greatest raid on the national wealth ever contemplated.

A man with a sense of history, Catton brilliantly anticipated the Great Giveaway. In two years the Administration has carried forward a giveaway program unmatched in our history, and the next two years may be more extravagant than the first. For despite stout opposition on some issues —the twelve-day filibuster on the atomic bill is a case in point—the Administration has every intention of going steadily forward with its giveaways. . . .

No one, of course, can reckon the total for the giveaways to date; only estimates are possible. Who knows the value of the underseas oil reserves? Is it ten billion dollars or thirty billion or three hundred billion? Who knows the value of atomic power?

> It is a fact [writes Senator Herbert H. Lehman] that in the unleashed energy of the atom there is more power potential than that contained in all of the unmined coal in the United States, more than that contained in all of the developed and reserve oil pools in the United States, more than that produced by all the hydroelectric plants now in existence. . . . This is not a million-dollar giveaway or a billion-dollar giveaway. This is a giveaway of such proportions as to dwarf the imagination, and to beggar any numbers which are used to describe it.

However the sum is reckoned, one thing is clear: if the Republicans don't get in power for another twenty years, they have already succeeded in doing right well for themselves and their chief contributors. . . .

The Great Giveaway is quite unlike anything of the sort that we have known heretofore. It is not in the pattern of the Great Barbecue of the Grant Administration, and it would be even less realistic to say that it follows the pattern of events that unfolded when Harding and the Ohio gang took over in Washington. "Little black bags" [a reference to the satchel containing $100,000 sent to Secretary of the Interior Fall in the Teapot Dome oil scandal] have no part in the current giveaway. It is as misleading to think that the Great Giveaway is merely another in a long history of similar episodes as it is to believe that the current assault on civil liberties is "just another" episode like the Palmer raids [a series of raids upon homes and labor headquarters in 1919-1920 by Attorney General Palmer, who applied existing espionage and sedition laws to bring about the arrest, imprisonment, and deportation of large numbers of aliens].

This, so far as we know, is the first time that an Administration has come to power in Washington determined to give away all public assets not securely nailed down by constitutional or statutory provisions. In the past unscrupulous individuals and greedy interests, working impartially with Democratic and Republican Administrations, have used political influence to enrich themselves. In the past, however, individuals and interests have been the initiators, and they have usually exploited some weakness in government, as, say, a corrupt official. But today the government is the initiator. This is an Administration *dedicated* to the giveaway. It has actively sought out opportunities to dispose of assets and resources. It is not being used so much as it is seeking to be useful. Let's face it: the Great Giveaway of the Eisenhower Administration is based on principle. . . .

Republicans have somewhat different obligations than Democrats; they raise money at the top, the Democrats at the bottom. The corruption characteristic of the Truman Administration took the form of cases "fixed" by Internal Revenue officials, of cost-plus contracts granted on the suggestion of mysterious five percenters, of RFC [Reconstruction Finance Corporation] loans arranged for bankrupt concerns which retained the right lawyers and accountants. Indeed, all comparisons of this sort are likely to be misleading.

To understand the Great Giveaway one must take a look at the circumstances which set it in motion.

As the 1952 campaign approached, the Republicans began to look about for popular issues. Up to this time they had fumed and fussed about "big government," but apparently it had not occurred to them that crusades are usually organized not to defend something but to get something. Finally, by just working at the issue of "statism," like a dog worrying with a bone, they hit upon the idea of giving it a more affirmative emphasis by suggesting that "big government" had some things which might be given *back*, not to the people, but to certain people. It is one thing to resist "creeping socialism" defensively, mournfully, with an eye on the past, but the response is much better when the barkers step forward and shout "Come and get it!"

The first significant intimation of something new in Republican tactics was provided when Charles E. Wilson, former president of General Electric, came forth with a "plan to end socialism in the United States." The plan had the merit of simplicity: Mr. Wilson wanted the government to sell as many businesses, power projects, and the like as possible, and to apply the proceeds in reduction of the national debt. Dismissed as somewhat fanciful in some quarters, the suggestion was greeted with enthusiasm by the Republican brain-trusters. . . . Thrilled by these bold new vistas, various Republican spokesmen began to talk about the "profits" that might be realized from the sale of the Post Office franchise.

By the time of the inauguration interest in the "goodies" that the Administration had promised to distribute had become the major political passion among Republicans. "A new era is dawning," said *United States News & World Report* on May 1, 1953. Soon the Administration would begin to "desocialize" government. The tide of "socialism" which had crept up until the government found itself in possession of $130 billion worth of loans, insurance, factories, railroads, ships, and "countless other things" was about to turn. To inflame the imagination of the business executives among its readers, *United States News* prepared the following chart, which appeared under a dollar sign ($) caption:

UNCLE SAM'S BIGGEST BUSINESSES: HEADED FOR PRIVATE ENTERPRISE?

Insurance	
(face value, veterans' policies)	$49,354,000,000
Banking	
(loans to farmers, homeowners, miners, states, industries, cooperatives, foreign governments, etc.)	18,600,000,000
Armament factories	8,600,000,000
Stockpile of strategic materials	5,845,000,000
Merchant shipping	4,000,000,000
Atomic facilities	3,800,000,000
Electric power	3,660,000,000
Housing, community facilities	1,064,000,000
Surplus farm products, U. S. owned	1,123,000,000
Synthetic rubber plants	750,000,000
Inland Waterways Corporation (barges)	27,000,000

As though stunned by the very boldness of the concept, the editors did not compute the total: $96,823,000,000, or, roughly, a hundred billion dollars.

Once in power, the Republicans set about preparing a more complete inventory of what was available for giveaways other than the major items of the type listed above, of which everyone was aware. By June 1953, the House Committee on Government Operations could report, in a preliminary way, that the government had become the nation's largest insurer, electric-power producer, lender, landlord, grain owner, warehouse operator, and shipowner, and that it monopolized the world's biggest potential new industry—atomic energy. . . . By midsummer, 1953, business executives had begun to worry about the "inventory recession" and were eager to find new business opportunities. As though by magic a strong pressure campaign got under way to compel Congress to turn over some of these highly advertised plums to private business. Indeed, the first business giveaway—

of the Mississippi barge lines . . . was consummated within a week after the committee's first inventory was released.

The big government enterprises like TVA did not, of course, need to be advertised; for these items eager bidders were standing by. What the House committee did was to whet the appetites of the "little business men," who were quite as eager as the big ones to get a slice of whatever it was that this Administration wanted "to give back." As its hearings continued, all sorts of new opportunities were unearthed. It was discovered that the government manufactured paint and rope, roasted coffee, made spectacles, dentures, and wooden legs, stored furniture, ran tugboats, repaired office furniture, cleaned windows, processed ferrous scrap, manufactured wooden boxes, operated supermarkets, sold liquor, and did all sorts of other things that might better be done, or so it seemed, by private business, for a profit. The big fat giveaways are of course the major concern . . . but a word or two about the minor ones which have been held out, as lure, for the small fry helps to underscore the meaning of the Great Giveaway.

In each instance an organized pressure group brought the initial complaint of "creeping socialism" to the attention of the House committee. Thus the Cordage Institute complained of the Navy's famous ropewalk in Boston (established in 1828). The National Paint, Varnish and Lacquer Association complained bitterly of the Navy's equally famous paint-manufacturing establishments (founded in 1902). The National Retail Liquor Package Stores Association felt as outraged as the Women's Christian Temperance Union over the sale of package liquor in officers' clubs. The National Wooden Box Association called attention to the government's box-manufacturing plants. And the International Association of Ice Cream Manufacturers reported that the government was making ice cream, and of all flavors too, in exactly 162 locations. And so it went.

As the hearings went on, anxious retailers, worried about dwindling sales, began to grow pop-eyed with wonder, like youngsters staring at store windows full of Christmas toys and gadgets, when they learned of a far-flung system of Post Exchanges in which government personnel can buy, at remarkably low prices, many items other than necessities— everything, in fact, from earrings to salt shakers. In 1948, the last year for which complete figures are apparently available, 375 such exchanges did a business of $250 million. But the investigators were also brought up hard by some unpleasant facts. They had to admit, for example, the existence of something called "military socialism," which, more than any other factor perhaps, accounts for "creeping socialism" of the PX variety. And they were soon forced to realize, that, on a strict cost basis, it would be difficult for private business to compete with many of these government operations. The shrewder members of the committee must now realize that many of the "goodies" promised Main Street store owners will never be delivered. But this promised giveaway, whether or not it will ever be fulfilled, has helped to keep the small fry happy while big business has walked away with major items that were not securely nailed down. . . .

Seen in this perspective, the Great Giveaway has novel dimensions and aspects. For the last decade or so Congress has shown spasmodic interest in "reversing the trend toward socialism," but as Roger Stuart has pointed out in a recent series of articles for the Scripps-Howard newspapers, "until the present Administration came into being, relatively little was accomplished beyond mere talk." This Administration, however, is committed to a program of "rolling back" the trend toward socialism by giving away government assets and enterprises that private business might operate at a profit.

Admittedly this is a bold and ambitious program. . . . The Republicans, it must be emphasized, do not feel apologetic about the program; they are proud of it. They do not regard it as a "raid" on Federal resources; nor have they been "bribed" to execute it. As they see it, they are engaged in a great effort to rewrite twenty years of history. "The central theme of the Eisenhower Administration," according to Senator Karl Mundt, "in all of its policies and programs, is to expand the opportunities and to increase the freedoms . . . of Mr. John American." Back in 1952 this same Mr. John American told Senator Mundt: "I've had enough of 'take-away' government. I want a government which will 'give away' some of its authority and its power by placing it back in the hands of ordinary people of America."

This, then, in Republican language, is the program which the Administration is carrying out as rapidly as it can. In short, the "public" side of our economy is to be kept to a bare minimum; at the same time the "private" side is to be expanded at the expense of the public by taking over all that is giveable and profitable from the other. Basically, this is the domestic program of the Eisenhower Administration.

GIVE AWAY WHAT? [7]

During the last two years the long trend toward "big government" in the United States has been checked. In particular, Congress and the Administration have taken a series of steps to remove the government from the anomalous role of competitor against its own citizens in several fields of business enterprise. Usually these steps have been taken in the face of strenuous opposition, and in most cases the opposition has been spearheaded by the cry of "giveaway." Naturally, the same slogan has been used in the election campaign.

This is a serious charge. It amounts to an accusation the the government is taking what rightfully belongs to all the people and bestowing it upon a favored few. Any government that did such a thing would be guilty of a breach of trust and unworthy of the people's support. So it is important that the people should understand what lies behind the accusation—what, if anything, has been "given away," by whom, and to whom.

[7] From *Guaranty Survey*, published monthly by the Guaranty Trust Company of New York. 34:1-3. November 1954. Reprinted by permission.

The "Tidelands" Dispute

What was "given away" when Congress passed and the President signed the bill recognizing the states' claims to submerged lands—the so-called tidelands—within their historic boundaries? For a century such lands had belonged to the states under a settled rule of law, supported by numerous court decisions. The question did not assume major importance, however, until the late 1930's when rich oil resources were discovered off the coasts of a few states. The Federal Government promptly laid claim to these newly found riches, and the Supreme Court upheld the claim by a 4-to-3 vote, despite precedents to the contrary.

Congress, however, was not satisfied with the validity of the government's claim to the submerged lands, and three times it passed bills recognizing the states' ownership. The first two bills were vetoed by President Truman. The third was signed by President Eisenhower.

Was this a "giveaway" or merely the cancellation of a "takeaway," the reassertion of a time-honored right, and the repudiation of an act of confiscation? Did the discovery of oil under the submerged lands give the Federal Government a title to the lands which it had not possessed before and which it would probably not have thought of claiming if the oil had not been found there? Oil is an important natural resource, but so is all productive land. Does it follow that the Federal Government should seize all the land? The Socialist's answer might be "yes," but the traditional American answer is "no."

The essence of the "tidelands" controversy is states' rights *versus* Federal rights to leasing and royalty revenues. As far as the business community is concerned, it has been given nothing. It will have to pay leasing and royalty charges to the states, just as it would have had to pay them to the Federal Government. . . .

The Power Controversy

The Federal Government in the last twenty years has posed as a strong advocate of power development. Yet the efforts of private enterprise to undertake such development have been beset with governmentally created difficulties. It took five years for the Federal Power Commission and the Virginia Electric & Power Company to obtain a Supreme Court decision overriding the objections of the Interior Department to the private construction of a hydroelectric project at Roanoke Rapids, North Carolina. For three years the Departments of the Interior and Agriculture combined to oppose the plan of the Idaho Power Company to construct three hydroelectric power dams on the Snake River.

In these and other cases the opposition has been based on the desire of governmental agencies to do the job themselves. It was not power that was desired, but *"public"* power. The political shibboleth has been that natural resources belonging to the people must not be "given away" to private "interests."

A controversy has raged over the generation of power from the Niagara River under governmental or private auspices. In the 1950 treaty with Canada, Congress reserved the authority to approve any project for the development of the United States' share of the power. The House of Representatives has voted in favor of the application of five private power companies in New York State. The principal opposition comes from the adherents of a plan to allow the New York State Power Authority, a governmental body, to undertake the development of power from the river.

The arguments offered in favor of the Authority's plan are the usual ones: that governmental operation would reduce the cost of energy to the consumer, and that a natural resource belonging to the people should be developed by the people.

The argument that governmental operation would reduce the cost of power is frequently supported by the contention that a governmental agency saves the cost of the taxes which would have to be paid by the private producer. This is spurious, for the state must have its revenue, and what is not collected in one form must be collected in another. If all the people as taxpayers are required to subsidize "cheap" power for some, where is the saving? Is it not obvious that the material gain which accrues to the people from a power development is determined by the cost of producing the power, not by the price at which it is sold by a subsidized state monopoly? And when we turn to the matter of construction and operating costs, does not experience with bureaucratic organization suggest that private managerial undertakings are likely to be more efficient?

The assertion that a natural resource belonging to the people should be developed by the people raises a more fundamental question. Since the people as a whole can never actively develop a resource, the assertion actually amounts to saying that a natural resource belonging to the people should be developed by their government. This may be fine-sounding to some, but its implications are socialistic and hence at odds with traditional American practice. Ours is a private-enterprise economy. The American people have decided that some things—such as postal service and primary education—must be carried on by government, but at the same time we have recognized that the general welfare is best served by minimizing government's role.

"Public power" is sometimes defended on the ground that it can be developed in conjunction with irrigation, flood control and other improvements not suitable for private enterprise. Whatever its merits may be, this argument has no application to the Niagara project, which is a matter of power and nothing else. Even where other types of improvement are involved, experience shows that these tend to become an entering wedge for governmental participation in business operations.

The Atomic Energy Act

The "giveaway" clamor reached its greatest height in the debate on the atomic-energy bill. The infant science and technology of atomic physics was developed on governmental initiative and by a huge expenditure of governmental funds. Why should its great potentialities for peaceful industrial use be "given away" to private business enterprise?

The law is limited incentive legislation, not "giveaway." It terminates the iron-clad governmental monopoly created by the Atomic Energy Act of 1946 and takes an initial step toward assimilating nuclear technology into the pattern of private enterprise. The change promises to accelerate the immense amount of work that must be done before atomic science can begin to realize its great potentialities. Experience teaches that progress is most rapid when men are actuated by incentives to put forth great efforts, bear heavy costs and assume large risks.

The new Atomic Energy Act retains abundant governmental safeguards against excessive private freedom in atomic development—so many, in fact, that the question arises whether it allows enough scope to private initiative to produce the desired results. It requires Federal licenses for the construction and operation of atomic-energy plants. It provides for exclusive Federal ownership of atomic materials and allows private enterprise only to lease these from the government. It permits the Atomic Energy Commission to continue research and experimentation in industrial as well as military uses of atomic energy, and to advance the art through construction of reactors of a development character which will result in limited amounts of power generation. It allows other Federal agencies to sell electric power produced from atomic energy in competition with private producers. It restricts the patent rights of inventors of new atomic processes.

As matters stand now, the door to private enterprise in atomic-energy development is only partially open. It may have to be opened a good deal wider before satisfactory progress can be made.

The new law "gives away" nothing. It rather grudgingly invites the people, acting on their individual initiative and in their individual interests, to participate in the development of a new industry that could bring incalculable benefits to all.

What the shouters of "giveaway" really dislike is the reassertion of the American tradition of private initiative and private enterprise. What they implicitly oppose is private profit, no matter how well earned the profit may be. What they actually desire is more governmental controls, greater centralization of power, deeper penetration of political authority into the lives of the people.

II. HYDROELECTRIC POWER

EDITOR'S INTRODUCTION

The battle of public versus private electric power was fought on many fronts during the first half of the Eisenhower Administration, and culminated finally in the signing of the highly controversial Dixon-Yates contract a few days after the congressional elections of 1954. At this writing, the Dixon-Yates dispute is still far from settled, and "The ABC's of Dixon-Yates," which follows immediately, outlines the controversy from the beginning, drawing a comparison of the Dixon-Yates plan with the proposed TVA expansion in facilities. In the second selection President Eisenhower gives his reason for favoring the private utility contract, and in the third Senator Kefauver explains why he opposes it.

In much broader terms, the Secretary of the Interior then outlines the Republican party's over-all policy on electric power. The three selections which follow Secretary McKay's statement discuss the issue of public versus private power for Hell's Canyon in the Northwest, and for expansion of TVA's power facilities.

THE ABC'S OF "DIXON-YATES" [1]

Almost overnight, the words "Dixon-Yates" are bobbing up from one end of the country to the other. President Eisenhower uses them. They're heard in Congress. People almost everywhere wonder what they're all about.

Edgar H. Dixon is the president of one private utility system and Eugene A. Yates is the chairman of the board of

[1] Article in *United States News & World Report.* 37:27-9. November 19, 1954. Reprinted from *United States News & World Report,* an independent weekly news magazine on national and international affairs published at Washington, D.C. Copyright 1954, United States News Publishing Corporation.

directors of another. They're in the limelight just now because they offered to build and operate a power plant to supply electricity for this country's atomic-energy program.

Argument that has flared around Mr. Dixon and Mr. Yates concerns their contract to supply power. This contract is one that directly raises the issue of public vs. private power. That is true not because of the contract's terms which, as now written, are substantially similar to power contracts made earlier, but rather because of the contract's bearing on the future of the Tennessee Valley Authority, the outstanding example of a public power agency in the United States.

The Dixon-Yates story really began a year ago, although at that time nobody had heard the term, and the partnership that bears the name had not been formed.

In December 1953 the Administration faced this dilemma: It had either to approve a new power plant for the TVA or to reduce TVA's orders for power.

As the principal source of electric power in the Southeast, TVA was beset with rising demands for energy. TVA figured that it was committed, under agreements with the Atomic Energy Commission and its regular customers, to provide about 600,000 more kilowatts of electric power per year, by 1957. It had to have another power plant to meet those commitments, and it wanted to build that plant at Fulton, Tennessee, near Memphis, because most of the new power demand was arising in Memphis.

President Eisenhower already had knocked out of the Federal budget the first TVA request for the new plant at Fulton, in the spring of 1953. By December 1953 his opposition to the new plant for TVA was stronger than ever.

Thus it was that the President—in December 1953—told the AEC to reduce its demands on the TVA system by getting a private power company to supply 600,000 kilowatts a year. That was the beginning of the Dixon-Yates story.

The second phase of Dixon-Yates now opened. Lewis Strauss, Chairman of AEC, set out to find 600,000 kilowatts of power for the AEC program.

Eventually, two companies headed by Mr. Dixon and Mr. Yates came up with a joint proposal for building a 650,000-kilowatt plant in West Memphis, Arkansas, which is just across the Mississippi River from Memphis.

This joint proposal was made on February 25, 1954. That is the birth date of Dixon-Yates as a national issue.

Three government agencies—the AEC, the Federal Power Commission and the TVA—now began to look over the initial Dixon-Yates proposal. This was done behind closed doors. But stories soon began to circulate in Washington that the government was being "taken." And TVA officials began to complain to their friends in Washington that they were being shown only part of the data relating to the proposed contract.

That was when supporters of the Tennessee Valley Authority, already on their mettle because of the rejection of the Fulton steam-plant project, began to see in the Dixon-Yates negotiations a direct attack on TVA—and a promising political issue that could embarrass the Administration in the coming 1954 election and call into question its whole basic power policy.

Commenting on the initial February 25 proposal, a member of the Dixon-Yates negotiating team says: "Frankly, our figures were too high." The AEC, the Federal Power Commission and the TVA came to the same conclusion. The initial Dixon-Yates proposal was rejected on March 24. The Dixon-Yates group then presented, on April 10, a revised proposal.

At this point, the AEC made another move that TVA supporters interpreted as an attack on TVA. AEC Chairman Strauss wrote to the Budget Bureau stating that AEC believed the TVA should bear the extra cost of any power bought by AEC to replace power originally scheduled to be furnished by TVA.

The Problem: To provide 600,000 kilowatts of electric power per year in west Tennessee for Federal power customers, including the Atomic Energy Commission

DIXON-YATES PROPOSAL

TVA PROPOSAL

PLANT:

Contract with Mississippi Valley Generating Company to build a steam power plant at West Memphis, Arkansas, MVGC is a new company formed by Middle South Utilities, Inc. (Edgar H. Dixon, president), and The Southern Company (Eugene A. Yates, chairman of the board).

Let Tennessee Valley Authority build a steam plant at Fulton, Tennessee. TVA is a government corporation, set up in 1933 to develop the Tennessee River Valley, run power projects created by flood-control dams.

COST:

$107,250,000 (estimate by Dixon-Yates group).

Approximately $100,000,000 (TVA estimate).

FINANCING:

Middle South and the Southern Company agree to put up $5,500,000, and borrow about $102,000,000 from banks and private investors—secured by bonds paying an estimated 3.5 per cent interest for 30 years.

United States Treasury would put up the $100,000,000 when appropriated by Congress. Treasury would borrow the money from the public at an estimated rate of 2.5 per cent.

WHAT AEC WOULD PAY FOR POWER:

$21,389,000 a year, of which government would recover $820,000 a year in income tax. Net cost to United States: $20,569,000.

$16,884,000 a year. TVA pays no Federal income tax.

Extra cost to government, of MVGC power, would be $3,685,000 a year. Of this: $1,499,000—taxes to state of Arkansas and city of West Memphis; $1,059,000—higher interest cost of private-issue bonds over Federal bonds; $607,000—extra cost of transmitting power across Mississippi River; $520,000—higher allowance, by Dixon-Yates, for fuel, operating costs.

TVA pays no state and local taxes on power sold to Federal agencies.
TVA itself pays no interest on money borrowed by Treasury for TVA.
TVA's proposed dam would be closer to AEC plant at Paducah, Kentucky.
TVA's lower fuel costs might be matched by MVGC, but no one is sure.

PROFITS:

As proposed, charges allow a 9 per cent return, or $495,000 a year, on Dixon-Yates investment. Charges also allow for usual commissions on sale of bonds; interest on bonds, repayment of bonds in 30 years.

TVA pays its operating costs, plus depreciation, and earns 4 per cent on government's investment, as represented by appropriations for power projects. Some of earnings go to repay appropriations over a 40-year period.

AFTER 25 YEARS

MVGC would own the plant. But government, at any time, could have canceled its power order, on payment of a penalty.

TVA would own the plant. TVA estimates it will need more power for regular industrial and home consumers regardless of what happens to AEC.

The Basic Question: A choice between two philosophies toward power.

Under Dixon-Yates proposal, private industry, instead of government's TVA, gets a job to do. It's a boost for private power.

Under TVA proposal, another steam plant is added to growing network of TVA plants. Public power gets a boost.

This letter was not made public at the time, but word of AEC's attitude got around. TVA officials estimated that the Dixon-Yates contract, because of subsidiary arrangements it would entail between AEC and TVA, would cost the TVA $3,750,000 a year, while blocking TVA's chance to get a new steam plant and "invading" its market area with 600,000 kilowatts of privately produced power.

All this hit TVA just at the time when its appropriations were being cut by the House below President Eisenhower's recommendations. To TVA and its friends, it looked as though the Tennessee Valley Authority was being scuttled from all directions.

The third phase, open political warfare over Dixon-Yates, now began. Mr. Dixon and Mr. Yates, not themselves parties to the differences between TVA and AEC, found themselves caught in the backlash of argument and recrimination.

Cries of skulduggery went up from Capitol Hill. Tennessee congressmen charged that the Dixon-Yates proposal was a covert attack on TVA, intended to start the "dismemberment" of the TVA service area. But Senator J. W. Fulbright (Democrat), of Arkansas, welcomed the contract as bringing tax revenue and a big annual payroll to his state, and declared that the contract was justified in the national interest.

That's how Dixon-Yates became the subject of headlines and bitter debate in Congress. . . . Yet the contract itself between the Dixon-Yates combine and the AEC had not been written when most of the debate took place. The actual contract was being hammered out, in July and August [of 1954], behind closed doors at the AEC by a team of eight utility executives on one side and ten AEC officials on the other.

Signing of the contract became the next point of controversy, in the fourth, most recent, phase of the story.

During this period, AEC and TVA composed most of their differences over the contract. Brigadier General Herbert D. Vogel, appointed head of TVA by President Eisenhower to succeed Gordon Clapp, a Democratic appointee, announced on September 3 that a meeting of minds had been reached with AEC. He said that additional costs of new power resulting from the Dixon-Yates contract would not go into TVA's cost structure or be reflected in its basic power rates, which have been used as a "yardstick" in measuring private utility charges.

After another skirmish in Congress, before the Joint Committee on Atomic Energy, the contract was modified again, to limit Dixon-Yates profits to a maximum of $600,000 a year and to include several other provisions deemed favorable to the government. Then the AEC signed the contract.

The Dixon-Yates proposal, as it compares in major points with the TVA's proposal, is outlined in the accompanying chart. It costs the government more money, per year, than TVA's plan. But it avoids a Federal capital outlay of $100 million and the risk of having a power plant it doesn't need at some future date. TVA says that's no risk, because it could use the new plant for sure.

The issue, in any case, now is joined between public and private power. As President Eisenhower sees it, the Dixon-Yates contract is the best deal that was offered the government. As supporters of TVA see it, the contract is the first step in a campaign to hem in, perhaps destroy, the TVA. Thus, Dixon-Yates seems certain to be an issue for some time to come.

THE PRESIDENT ON "DIXON-YATES" [2]

Dear Stub:

On several occasions you and I have discussed the Administration plan to relieve TVA of part of its obligation to furnish electric power to AEC in order that TVA, without additional steam plants built at taxpayers' expense, may have an adequate supply of electric power for its customers through 1957.

[2] Text of a letter from President Dwight D. Eisenhower to Representative W. Sterling Cole (Republican, New York), chairman of the Joint Congressional Atomic Energy Committee, on the Dixon-Yates contract. New York *Herald Tribune.* p 19. November 11, 1954.

My general thinking on the subject is this: It seems to me that all arguments for the construction by the Federal Government of the additional steam plants ignore this one and very important truth: if the Federal Government assumes responsibility in perpetuity for providing the TVA with all the power it can accept, generated by any means whatsoever, it has a similar responsibility with respect to every other area and region and corner of the United States of America.

Logically, every section of the United States should have the same opportunities, and the Federal Government should not discriminate between the several regions in helping to provide this type of facility. My own conviction is that we have not been alert enough in making certain of this equality of treatment. If this is the case, then it is high time that other regions were getting the same opportunities.

I cannot believe that Americans, in general, disapprove of attempting to place all regions on a basis of equality in this regard. Consequently, there must either be some reexamination of any plans which would call for the Federal Government to supply all the additional power capacity that might be needed in the future in the Tennessee Valley or logically we would have to begin plans for a gigantic power development to cover the entire nation equitably.

The directive to the AEC to make arrangements for the purchase of private power—either directly or by finding a new private source to replace available TVA power—was designed to allow time for a thorough examination of this whole vast field, without hurting the citizens of the valley.

As a consequence of these facts, I believe that the project for building new plants at Federal expense—implying a purpose of continuing this process indefinitely in the future —is therefore wholly indefensible unless it should become part of a vast national plan. If this is to be national policy, it is most certainly a project that demands earnest and prayerful study. In the meantime, the citizens of that region will not be deprived of the additional power they need for the next several years.

It seems to me that there has been a very great deal of talk and argument—much of it partisan—about issues that are really clear and simple. No one in this Administration has any intention of destroying or damaging TVA or of diminishing its effectiveness in any way. But this is not the same thing as fastening on the Federal Government a continuing and never-ending responsibility which I frankly do not believe is logical nor, in the long run, in the best interests of the country.

The Administration plan and all facts concerning its development have been before the public for months. I hope that the Joint Atomic Energy Committee will give the plan, and the proposed contract to carry it into effect, the fullest consideration that the committee deems necessary. If, however, after such consideration, the committee is of the opinion that the final contract terms are completely satisfactory, it would be clearly desirable and in the best interests of the people of the TVA area that any additional waiting periods be waived, so that construction may begin as soon as possible and people in the TVA area may make their plans for the future.

With warm personal regard, sincerely,

DWIGHT D. EISENHOWER.

"DIXON-YATES": THE DEMOCRATIC PARTY'S VIEW [3]

The people in the seven-state region of the Tennessee Valley, and a growing number of others all over the nation are increasingly disturbed by the Dixon-Yates deal. . . .

It had its inception in the Administration's hatred of TVA and its misguided conception of what constitutes "free enterprise."

Two years ago the Tennessee Valley Authority proposed in its budget the construction of a new steam generating

[3] Statement by Senator Estes Kefauver (Democrat, Tennessee), prepared at the request of the New York *Herald Tribune*. New York *Herald Tribune*. p 1+. October 16, 1954. Reprinted by permission.

plant at Fulton, Tennessee, in order to meet the growing power needs—both domestic and defense—of the valley.

The then new Eisenhower Administration, fresh from the campaign during which the President had promised continued operation of TVA at "maximum efficiency," deferred action on this proposal pending a "study" of the power needs of the valley.

Presumably this "study"—which Budget Director Dodge admitted was being made in consultation with officials of the Edison Electric Institute, a propaganda wing of the private power organization—confirmed TVA's own estimates. For this year, admitting that the need existed, the Administration came up with a proposal to solve that need "without adding to the public debt." Their plan was the Dixon-Yates deal. This is how it works:

Two utility holding companies—Middle South Utilities, headed by Mr. Dixon, and the Southern Company, headed by Mr. Yates—would join together and build a 650,000 kilowatt plant at West Memphis, Arkansas.

The Atomic Energy Commission would contract with this plant for all its power. However, the power would not be delivered to AEC. Instead it would be delivered to TVA at Memphis, Tennessee, across the Mississippi River from West Memphis, Arkansas. There the power would go into the regular TVA system, lighting the homes and turning the wheels of industry at Memphis—but theoretically it would be "replacement" for a similar amount of power being furnished by TVA to AEC at Paducah, Kentucky.

In other words, the plan would distort the functions of AEC from splitting the atom to power brokering, which three of the five AEC commissioners thought was a bad idea in itself, and said so publicly. Of course, the TVA directors opposed it.

I shall always remember a meeting of a Senate Appropriations subcommittee which I attended. . . . The opposition of directors and commissioners of these two "independent" agencies had been expressed. The committee heard testimony showing that there had been no advertisement for bids on the West Memphis plant and no competitive bids received—that, in fact, a group of New York financiers who desired to compete were frozen out of competition.

Then absolute proof was presented that the Dixon-Yates proposal would cost the taxpayers—who pay all the AEC power bills—between $92 million and $140 million more over the life of the contract than would the same power from TVA.

As the hearings were in progress, General K. D. Nichols, general manager of AEC, received a letter from the Budget Bureau. It stated "the President directs" the AEC to enter into immediate final negotiations with the Dixon-Yates group for the power. . . .

In the space that I have it would be impossible to detail everything I think is wrong with this policy and this contract, but just let me make a few generalizations:

1. This is supposed to be done in the name of "a return to free enterprise"—but this proposed contract is a far cry from "free enterprise." At least two of the most important elements are missing—namely, competition and risk. There was no competitive bidding. There is absolutely no risk involved. In one of its drafts, the proposal even exempted the company from all taxes, state and local as well as Federal. In addition, the company will be guaranteed a profit.

2. It will unite two holding companies, each of which already exerts monopolistic control over the vital power supply of a large part of the South and Southeast, into one gigantic enterprise with influence and power of staggering proportions.

3. It is in the interest of the government for TVA to survive—because this agency (unlike the Dixon-Yates combine) repays the government every cent invested in power operations over a forty-year period. In order to be able to operate efficiently, and keep up that repayment schedule, it must have control of its own power supply.

Finally, I cannot help but observe that this is the first time anybody in Washington ever did dictate to the regionally operated Tennessee Valley Authority—and never was there a dictation more resented by the "local people" to whom the Administration pays such frequent lip service.

Unfortunately, this Dixon-Yates deal is not an isolated example. In fact, the weakening of TVA is just a part of the larger "giveaway" program which includes such valuable assets as the offshore oil reserves, the exploitation of atomic energy, and the benefits from other power projects stretching from Niagara Falls to the Central Valley of California, from Clark Hill on the Georgia-Carolina line to Bonneville and Hell's Canyon in the great Northwest.

NEW POLICY ON ELECTRIC POWER [4]

Q. Why do you feel that it is necessary for the Federal Government to develop any power projects, Secretary McKay? Why shouldn't the whole development be left to private enterprise?

A. In the construction of large, multiple-purpose dams, particularly in the Northwest and the Missouri Basin—and perhaps there are some in the Southwest—it's impossible for private enterprise or local public agencies to do the job.

Q. What do you mean by multiple purpose?

A. Irrigation, navigation, flood control and power. That is, a multiple-purpose dam is one into which is built all of these features. In most cases private-enterprise people or a public agency have no way of charging off the costs for irrigation or navigation or flood control.

Q. So it's necessary to have the government do some of the development?

A. Yes. But our idea is not to be in competition or not to try to create a government monopoly. I don't like monopoly of any kind, but the worst type is monopoly by the Federal Government, because it's so hard to change. Private

[4] From interview by the editors of *United States News & World Report* with Secretary of the Interior Douglas McKay. *United States News & World Report.* 35:62-6+. October 9, 1953. Reprinted from *United States News & World Report,* an independent weekly news magazine on national and international affairs published at Washington, D.C. Copyright 1953, United States News Publishing Corporation.

enterprise can be controlled by regulatory bodies. The change can be controlled by regulatory bodies. The change we hope to bring about is a cooperative effort by the local people. We want to see locally owned private utilities and locally managed utilities cooperate to develop power, and the Federal Government do only the things that are necessary, instead of trying to take over the whole field.

Q. Is there a feeling that there isn't capital enough, that private enterprise cannot put up enough capital?

A. No, I don't think there is any question about capital, because the money can be raised. But the question is how are you going to collect revenues and pay it back. You see, in a multiple-purpose dam there are no reimbursable items, such as flood control. It is impossible to collect any revenue for that.

Q. That is a function of the government, isn't it?

A. That's right.

Q. After the government builds the dam, do you think it should step aside and the transmission lines be left to private companies to build?

A. There are two schools of thought on this, and my idea is, of course, down the middle of the road. I don't believe under any circumstances the government should build transmission lines to compete with those lines already constructed. That's economically unsound.

Q. Is that actually being done?

A. Oh yes, that has been done in power administration in some cases. In cases where the Federal Government wishes to move power over lines of a private company, it can make a "wheeling" contract with a private utility. Why shouldn't it, provided the utility will give the service on a reasonable basis?

There might be a case, or cases, where private enterprise becomes unreasonable, and in such a case you might have to build Federal transmission lines.

Q. Don't they sell any power to private companies in the Tennessee Valley?

A. No, they are short of power now because they have developed all the hydroelectric energy that can be developed to take care of the peak loads, and now they need steam-generating plants. However, that is not my jurisdiction.

Q. You think the TVA model is wrong?

A. In my opinion it is definitely wrong. I appeared in Washington before Congress in 1949, together with three other governors of the Northwest, on a bill to set up a Columbia Valley Administration which was under consideration. We opposed a CVA. We didn't want anything to do with it. It is a philosophy of government.

I am opposed, violently opposed, to a central government which tells the people out in Oregon how they shall live. We have been living there for more than a hundred years—that is, my people have. They were out there before there was any government, and through the years they seem to have gotten along all right. We don't want anybody in Washington telling us in detail what is best for our own good.

Q. You mean you opposed the CVA as such, not simply the CVA system?

A. My opinion on public power is this: We have public power out in my state. We have it in the Federal Government, and we have it in public-utility districts, and we have it in municipally owned operations. We have had one in Eugene, Oregon, for thirty-five years. It is very successful. It was started out by businessmen and run as a business organization.

If the people in my community want to have their power as a public ownership, I have no quarrel with them. I do resent some planner promoting a program for the people out there—or anywhere else, for that matter—to force this issue by the Federal Government on the local people. I just don't like it. I have said time and again there is room for both public and private power in this nation. People have at their command machinery to obtain public ownership, and I would never stand in the way of such a program.

Q. Is the government now in the business of distributing power as well as making power in the Northwest?

A. Oh, yes. Take the Bonneville Power Administration —it is unique. We have a Northwest Power Pool. All the power developed by all the agencies—public-utility districts, municipal, privately owned utilities and the Bonneville Power Administration—is dumped into a single power pool and distributed to the users.

We have a board that runs this with representation from each of the Federal agencies, local power bodies and private companies concerned. It's been very successful.

Now I say we could be in a partnership like this, working together, without throwing any rocks in the paths of private enterprise. There has been too much propaganda about public ownership. And by the same token I feel that the million customers of the privately owned power companies—little people, homeowners, farmers, small businessmen —have some right in this world as well as big business and public-ownership groups.

With that thought in mind I am negotiating a twenty-year contract with private utilities in the Pacific Northwest who are customers of the Bonneville Power Administration. By the same token I feel there must be equity in the distribution of Federal power, and that equity must extend all the way down the line.

Q. What you need is more power, really, isn't it?

A. Yes. You see the country out there is growing so rapidly, and is changing from an agricultural to an industrial economy. Because of the low cost of power out there, some of the large chemical and aluminum companies and other metals companies have been attracted to the region. In World War II the government came out there to build more aluminum plants. We produced 35 to 40 per cent of all the aluminum in America from its plants because of that cheap power.

As we continue to expand, it will attract more people for that kind of business. It is the type of business which requires tremendous loads of electric energy.

Q. How are you going to expand—through government investment or private investment?

A. Both.

Q. You don't object to some government dams then.

A. No, I would say this, that at present we haven't the money for any new starts on any new dams. In 1950 President Truman called a halt on new starts when the Korean war broke out. This should have been done because the first thing you have got to do is insure the defense of the nation.

The big job today is to balance the Federal budget so that we can again live within our means. When the picture changes, in my opinion, this country must continue to be interested, as it has always been, in the natural resources of America, and to do the things that the people at home can't do for themselves—the promotion of reclamation, irrigation, flood control and power from multiple-purpose dams.

THE BATTLE FOR HELL'S CANYON [5]

Very few people have ever seen Hell's Canyon. Except for a weekly mail boat, the canyon, which is the deepest river cleft in America, is isolated from civilization—and looks in fact like a displaced region of another, wilder planet. Scarred and brutal bluffs of volcanic ash cut in some places as deep as seven thousand feet down to the churning Snake River, which forms the northern half of the Oregon-Idaho line. . . .

Remote as it is, Hell's Canyon, one of America's last great power sites, is being fought over in the most momentous power fight since the late Wendell Willkie took on TVA.

The issue arose . . . when the Interior Department under its new Republican leadership withdrew as intervener before the Federal Power Commission, the body empowered to decide what kind of dam could be built on the Snake River—

[5] From article by Joe Miller, a Seattle writer who has been covering hydroelectric power developments in the Northwest for several years. *Reporter.* 10: 23-7. May 11, 1954. Reprinted by permission.

one multipurpose high Federal dam or three relatively small dams to be built by the Idaho Power Company.

The argument between public power and private power is an old one, but the regional and national interest that Hell's Canyon has aroused in the past year is a matter of considerable surprise to both sides. . . . [Last year] the working advocates of a big dam were a corporal's guard concentrated in northern Idaho and eastern Oregon. Today they are a small army stationed throughout the Northwest and extending into other regions as far away as New England. Along with the traditional farmer-labor nucleus, the army includes bank presidents, Idaho's biggest Republican fund raiser, influential businessmen, and other stanch free enterprisers. "If we're Socialists," said an eastern Oregon chamber of commerce president, "then Norman Thomas had better reorganize his party because there are a lot of us."

Actually, both sides in this debate begin with the postulate that the Snake River and the entire Columbia River Basin must serve private enterprise. They differ only as to how it may best be served. The low dams would certainly show a profit for private enterprise, at least for the stockholders of the Idaho Power Company. The single high federally built dam would provide cheap power to a number of smaller private enterprises, as well as more extensive facilities for flood control, irrigation and reclamation, storage, and conservation.

The prize is a mighty one, and much more than Hell's Canyon is at stake. The Columbia system still has 10.2 million kilowatts to be developed. Decisions made now may well set the region's hydroelectric pattern for many years to come.

Background for the Battle

Lending an urgency to this struggle is the Northwest's pressing need for huge new resources of power, a minimum of 500,000 to 600,000 more kilowatts every year just to keep pace with growing consumer loads. And these figures do not include power for new industrial development. It would not be an exaggeration to say that the Northwest's economic future rests largely upon the outcome of this conflict.

The voices of the adversaries are loud and strong. The president of Washington's Public Utility Districts, Dan Jolly, thunders that the public power program is "being systematically scuttled." Private utility spokesmen declare that they can "develop the river faster and cheaper than the government."

The vast interest becomes explainable when you compare the Northwest of today with the Northwest of fifteen years ago. Cheap power has brought new plants, such as the Hanna Corporation's $50 million nickel plant at Roseburg, Oregon, and Harvey Machinery's $60 million aluminum factory at The Dalles, Oregon, to areas that were almost entirely agricultural a few years ago. Population has increased by almost 40 per cent; Seattle alone has jumped from 376,000 in 1940 to 544,000 today.

This flowering has produced a considerable change in the Northwest's economic attitudes. No longer relying solely on lumber, fish, and agriculture, business leaders now talk of aluminum (of which the area, starting from zero in 1940, now produces 44 per cent of the national supply), and of other new light metals, such as magnesium, titanium, and zirconium, whose fabrication requires great amounts of low-cost power. Because of its outstanding power potential, the Northwest envisions itself as the center of the burgeoning light-metals and electrochemical industries.

But the businessmen, at least many of them, are now in something of a quandary. As free-enterprise Republicans, they are dedicated to keeping the government out of the power business. And yet they see realistically that continued development of Federal low-cost power according to the multipurpose dam program initiated by Franklin D. Roosevelt is vital to the expansion of Northwest industry.

This poses a problem for the Eisenhower Administration, which has made quite plain its intention to create a climate favorable for business. To do this in the Northwest requires the continued development of low-cost power to create opportunities for industrial expansion. . . .

The Battle Begins

After the Interior Department abdicated . . . from active defense . . . favoring the construction of a single high dam at Hell's Canyon, people all over the country began to shout "giveaway." Bills supporting Hell's Canyon (introduced on the Senate side by Wayne Morse of Oregon and thirteen others, on the House side by Gracie Pfost (Democrat, Idaho) and Don Magnuson (Democrat, Washington) became focal points for supporters. . . . Within weeks a National Hell's Canyon Association had sprung into being. Support for the high dam has come blowing off the Northwest's farmlands into Washington with genuine nonpartisan spontaneity. . . .

Quiet support is also coming in from a number of businessmen, many of whom were outspokenly opposed to the earlier New Deal projects. Groups such as the Baker, Oregon, auto dealers have voted approval of the high dam. Others can't afford to be counted. "I can't speak publicly," said a bank president. "But if I had to testify on oath, my support would be for the high dam. It's a better deal."

To people such as this man, the issue is not political or ideological. It is practical. Hell's Canyon can provide the cheap power that would bring new industry to the Northwest. "While private enterprise is to be encouraged," commented the Salem, Oregon, *Statesman,* which is published by former Governor Charles Sprague, a Republican, "it should not disrupt plans of broader scope and importance. . . . Idaho Power will have a difficult time to sustain its case."

Those who argue for a high dam point out that the power plant would ultimately provide 1,124,500 kilowatts of power, 688,000 at the site and an additional 436,500 at downstream dams. That is more than one fourth of the Northwest's current total generation of four million kilowatts. Idaho Power's three dams would produce about 550,000 kilowatts, with no appreciable downstream generation. Upstream water storage increases the power potential of downstream dams by impounding water runoff in spring and summer and releasing water when needed in winter. Hell's

Canyon would have almost four times the storage capacity of the company dams. Without such storage capacity, it will be increasingly expensive to build other dams in the area, thus limiting its future growth.

The high dam would cost about $360 million, of which 88 per cent would be charged to power and paid back to the United States Treasury over a fifty-year period at 3 per cent interest. It would take five to seven years to build.

Integrating a river power system can make a great deal of difference in total output. For example, the pooling of the various Northwest power plants into one connected system enables these plants to generate 600,000 more kilowatts than they could by operating separately. "In the past it was the practice to build isolated projects on our rivers," Dr. Raver, the former chief at Bonneville, has said. "It captured but a small part of the river's usefulness. We have learned that by interconnecting all of the projects, it is possible to obtain larger benefits, creating a situation in which the whole is greater than the sum of its isolated parts."

Other regions of the country would stand to benefit from the Hell's Canyon project. One of the most important benefits would be low-cost phosphate fertilizer—urgently needed for soil restoration in many of the nation's farm areas. Southeastern Idaho contains fifty-two per cent of the nation's phosphate reserves. And yet these reserves have hardly been touched because it takes 4,350 kilowatt hours to produce one ton of phosphate for fertilizer, and that simply cannot be done profitably at Idaho Power's seven-mill rate. Three-mill Federal power from Hell's Canyon would make a ton of superphosphate $8.40 cheaper to produce.

Those who argue for Idaho Power's three-dam plan are equally sincere in their belief that what the Northwest needs is freedom for private enterprise in the power business.

Idaho Power, which serves 117,000 customers in eastern Oregon and southern Idaho, is—even its opponents in this case agree—a good company, in healthy financial condition. It has consistently grown, both in dollar value and kilowatt output. As a symbol of private enterprise, it is an excellent one and represents a formidable adversary in this conflict.

The company's argument runs this way: Its proposed rock-fill dams would cost only $133 million as compared to the $360 million for the high concrete dam. They would be finished in thirty-eight months, thus providing the power-hungry Northwest with the kilowatts it needs much sooner than the government could. Idaho Power would pay $10 million a year in taxes; the Federal dam would pay no taxes. Company witnesses have testified before the FPC [Federal Power Commission] that reputable investment houses can finance the dams and that a respected engineering company (Morrison-Knuden) can build them at the $133 million price. And finally, the company claims that there just isn't enough water in the Snake River to fill up a high-dam reservoir, a contention in which Washington's governor, Arthur B. Langlie, concurs.

Many of these arguments are hotly disputed. The backbone of the company's argument has always been that Federal power companies pay no taxes. The company's opponents point out first that the Bonneville Power Company makes substantial payments in lieu of taxes, and second, that the company has already requested tax-amortization certificates amounting to several million dollars.

John R. Riter, chief hydrologist of the United States Bureau of Reclamation, says that Idaho Power is wrong about the water supply: that there is enough to fill up a 607-foot dam with 3,880,000 acre-feet. The Snake's flow has been measured since 1923, and to avoid any doubts Riter took the low period from 1929 to 1937 as the basis for his analysis. He estimates that the high dam's reservoir would be more than adequate, since after it was once filled, the amount released in a year would always leave about one million acre-feet at the bottom as insurance for the low years. About 2.5 million feet would be released annually for downstream power generation, so that dams on the lower Columbia would have water passing through them at the crucial low periods when there have always been power shortages in the past.

To the farmers of southern Idaho, who have 2.6 million acres under irrigation, the high dam has been pictured as a threat. Unlike the situation in most of the Northwest, 60 to 70 per cent of Idaho's irrigation systems are owned by the farmers themselves. "You can have my wife, but don't mess with my water," is the way southern Idaho farmers are supposed to feel. Actually, the Morse-Pfost bill would safeguard these rights, but, persuaded that the Federal dam *would* mess with their water, many farmers have instinctively taken Idaho Power's side. "The three dams will protect our water rights," they seem to feel, "and to hell with the rest of the Northwest."

TRUST UNCLE SAM TO GET YOU A POWER SHORTAGE [6]

There are two areas in the United States that most particularly are always having power shortages. One is the area in the Southeast dominated by the electric system of the Federal Government's Tennessee Valley Authority. The other is that part of the Columbia River basin, in the Pacific Northwest, dominated by the Federal Government's Bonneville Power Administration.

The Columbia is a much mightier river than the Tennessee. It is much more capable of producing abundant power. It serves a region second to none for magnificence. So let us concentrate upon it. It is a star national lesson.

Imagine yourself the boss of the Bonneville Power Administration. In 1937 you are made selling agent for all the electricity from Federal dams constructed—or to be constructed—on the Columbia River or its tributaries. In 1939 you begin selling from your first dam, Bonneville, on the Columbia between Oregon and Washington. In 1941 you

[6] Article by William Hard, roving editor, *Reader's Digest*, and Charles Stevenson, department editor, *Reader's Digest*. *Reader's Digest*. 63:41-6. July 1953. Reprinted by permission.

begin selling from your second dam, the titanic Grand Coulee, also on the Columbia, in Washington.

You don't have to be much of a salesman to get customers. You are selling below-cost power. In the case of a privately owned electric company taxes are a necessary—and a considerable—part of cost. But you pay no taxes whatsoever, either Federal or local.

In 1941 you sell a billion kilowatt-hours of electric energy. In 1943 you sell five billion; in 1945, eight billion. But in 1946 you cannot meet the demands of your customers. And you announce another power shortage in 1947, another in 1948, still another in 1949.

The owners of a private utility would be dismayed. But you simply rush to Washington and roar at Congress:

"See my power shortage? Build me more dams!"

And Congress, bit by bit, seems to oblige. After a while there are eleven additional dams being started on the Columbia and on its tributaries, in Montana and Idaho as well as in Oregon and Washington. Your domain is now becoming really imperial. But within it, to your horror, there are a half-dozen private electric companies. To you they are nasty local monopolies. You aspire to enlarge, as fast as possible, into one great noble monopoly.

Under Federal law, in selling your electricity, you must give a "preference" to local electric agencies owned and operated by local governments. In Oregon and Washington there are local governmental units, known as Public Utility Districts, that deal in light and power. A great thought occurs to you:

"If I can enlarge the number of these Public Utility Districts, I can enlarge my sales."

Despite recurrent shortages, you send your agents to locality after locality and say:

"You are now served by a private electric company which generates and distributes its own power and also distributes the power I sell it. But I am not certain of having power to sell to that private company. I am thinking of cutting it off. I prefer to sell to a public agency. Want to be sure of getting electricity? Make yourselves into a Public Utility District, install a local distributing system and buy your power wholesale from me!"

Thus you move toward crippling the private electric companies and toward enlarging your own sales—and shortages.

But your thirst for overselling the beneficence of the Federal Government is not yet quenched. Your original mission was to sell electricity to local public agencies for distribution particularly to householders and farmers. You were to rescue "the domestic and rural consumer" from the grasp of "profit-seeking" private electric companies. But now you deliberately use your bait of below-cost power to attract into your area profit-seeking manufacturing corporations. A profit-seeking manufacturer of electricity is horrid. A profit-seeking manufacturer of aluminum is, somehow, nice.

So, presently, you have as the objects of your bounty the Aluminum Corporation of America, the Kaiser Aluminum and Chemical Corporation and the Reynolds Metals (aluminum) Company. A ton of aluminum, as it comes into being, is the biggest eater of electricity known to man. Yet, despite your shortage of power, you try to supply the electricity for about half of the pig-aluminum output of the country.

After a while you are getting about 45 per cent of your revenue from aluminum and other manufacturing enterprises.

Then in 1950, because of a continuous power shortage, the Assistant Secretary of the Interior comes to the Northwest and says:

"No new industries can get power in this area."

However, because of Korea the country needs still more aluminum. The businessman who heads the Defense Power Administration, operating within the Interior Department, holds that it will be dangerous to put more aluminum facilities into the power-short Pacific Northwest. The aluminum companies themselves prefer the Southwest, with its surplus supply of natural gas for fuel. But they reckon without Washington politics.

The Secretary of the Interior of 1951 is a vigorous proponent of Federal public power. He wants the new aluminum production to go to a Federal public-power area. Thereupon he overrules everybody and orders the new production —188,000 tons of it—into the Pacific Northwest.

As boss of the Bonneville Power Administration, you get this news at a moment when you are heading toward the climax of your power shortages. In the fall of 1951 you have to cut your service to industrial customers by hundreds of thousands of kilowatts. The voltages at your major substations drop to 75 per cent of normal. Some aluminum loads have to be dropped. *And for a time the Atomic Energy Commission's Hanford plant in your area has to be completely shut down.*

The trouble is that you have oversold the normal flow of the Columbia River. "The difficulty is that loads are beyond supply; we have to have substantially better than median flow to overcome the shortage," you confess to the press.

So what do you do? In 1952 you get yourself two more aluminum customers: the Anaconda Company in Montana and the Harvey Company in Oregon.

Then the Columbia really balks. In the winter of 1952-53 the lights on a lot of streets go dim. The aluminum companies have to reduce their output by a million pounds a day. The Defense Electric Power Administration has to tell all major consumers to cut down their power use by ten per cent. Many employees are laid off.

Citizens begin to ask why those new dams of yours don't get completed. Bob Jones, the chairman of the Utility Committee of Seattle, which has an outstanding public electric system, says:

"The Federal Government has taken on the responsibility of developing the Columbia River water resources. By doing so, it has made it difficult for our non-Federal agencies to finance new projects. . . . But for six years we have watched the continuous delays in Federal dam construction."

It is embarrassing. You can only explain that Federal dams will always lag behind the growing power demands of any region they dominate.

First you must get your dam "authorized." To do so, you must do a lot of lobbying in Washington. You must survive the scrutiny of the Budget Bureau and of House and Senate committees; you must survive debates on the floor of both Houses. All this sometimes takes years—and you have only begun.

You must next get an appropriation. Many dams have been authorized for years without getting an appropriation. Again you brave the Budget Bureau and committees of Senate and House. Again you anxiously coach your legislative friends on what to say in congressional debates. In the end, perhaps, you get your appropriation.

But you do not get an appropriation for all the time it takes to build the dam. No! You have to get a new appropriation every year. Every year you have to sweat in the old treadmill. And you virtually never get the amount of money you need.

So now you have a really bright idea. Besides the eleven dams under construction in your area, you have twelve dams authorized. You have failed to get appropriations for them. Forget them! You need something new and spectacular to make you again the savior of the Pacific Northwest.

You look eastward into southern Idaho, and see the Idaho Power Company, which furnishes power to 99 per cent of the farmers in its area. It is a very annoying company. It never has a power shortage, never. It has built seventeen power dams in the Snake River. Its policy is to expand in harmony with the area's expanding economic needs. So it has applied to the Federal Power Commission for a license to spend $130 million of its own money for new dams, said license to last for fifty years, during which these dams would produce almost half a billion dollars in taxes for the Federal Government and for Idaho.

Wicked! Another "grab" by the "Power Trust"! You denounce it and counterattack. You—that is, the Federal

Government—will build a new dam in the Snake, in a stupendous gorge called Hell's Canyon. It will drown out the proposed new dams of the Idaho Power Company. And what a dam, this new dream dam of yours! You spread publicity for it from coast to coast. It will be 1740 feet long, tower 722 feet into the sky! The second tallest dam in the universe! And costing only about half a billion dollars of taxpayers' money to build and put into operation. "Give me that dam," you say, "or else by 1960 there will be the most gosh-awful power shortage the Pacific Northwest has ever known!"

This year Hell's Canyon is the marching song of the Federal-power advocates in Congress. "If this Administration rejects Hell's Canyon," they intimate, "it will prove that it is against 'The People.' "

Meanwhile, an increasing number of "The People" in your area are accelerating their rebellion against Federal domination. The rebels include many advocates of local municipal public power. For instance, the commissioner of Tacoma's municipal electric system asks: "Is Tacoma to maintain an independent position in the service of electric energy in its own homes and industries or is it to become a mere cat's paw in a gigantic system of Federal power supply under rules dictated from Washington?"

So municipalities are by-passing you and going to the Federal Power Commission in Washington for licenses to dam neighboring streams. So are Public Utility Districts. One district is building the Box Canyon Dam on the Pend Oreille. But the truly amazing local ambition is at Priest Rapids on the Columbia.

At that site a Federal dam is authorized and its power is scheduled to be sold by your Bonneville Power Administration. But the Grant County Public Utility District now wants to build that dam itself, presumably with the help of other neighboring local public and private utility systems. It has applied to the Federal Power Commission for a license. The project will cost more than $300 million. If the plan goes through, Priest Rapids will be the first outsize multiple-purpose dam ever built by local efforts in the Pacific Northwest.

And now the state of Washington has passed a law which, from the Federal-power point of view, is outright sedition. This law, signed by Governor Langlie last March, makes it possible for all of Washington's power agencies, state and local, public and private, to work together for regional initiative in promoting power development and distribution.

Will this new machinery of grassroots self-government be able to control the Northwest's power shortages? Several years must pass before we can know the answer. Just one thing is sure:

Power development by the Federal Government has been guided by Federal ambitions, and has been high in promises and low in deliveries.

The only corrective in sight is power development by local people who know local needs and who will act in harmony with those needs. . . .

So let's go basic. The managers of . . . the Bonneville Power Administration have been devoted, diligent and enthusiastic—seemingly overenthusiastic—in their selling of cheap power. But suppose they now restrain their enthusiasm and become cold, perfect executives. They will still be handicapped in comparison with the executives of privately owned companies. Why? Because their supreme board of directors is the Congress. And the Congress can take years to do what the directors of a private company can often do in a day.

The appropriation processes of the Congress, we repeat, are characterized by protracted hearings and debates, by delayed decisions which must always be behind the rapid, instant needs of a growing business enterprise; and they will forever continue to exhibit that tardiness as long as America is America and as long as the Congress has not become the blind, dumb tool of an executive autocracy. Congress was built for political freedom, not for economic efficiency. By its very nature it can never display economic efficiency.

So to all regions of the United States not yet dominated by a Federal electric light and power system:

Want a power shortage? You now know how to get it.

DON'T LET TVA BE WRECKED, MR. PRESIDENT! [7]

MR. PRESIDENT:

To those of us in the Valley who have to do with it, the Tennessee Valley Authority means the democratic action of the people of a region, in partnership with the Federal Government, to conserve and develop the resources of that region for their own and the nation's use. . . .

Conception of the TVA Act was typically American and democratic. It was not, as some have supposed, *struck full-grown from the brow* of some New Deal brain-truster. It originated with Congress. It is the product of thirty-odd years of trying to harness the public interest and private enterprise, of worrying and wrangling, of trial-and-error procedure. . . .

I might say that over these years, the members of Congress—and Republican Congresses they were—as they exhausted one recourse after another to protect the public interest under some plan for private operation, gradually shifted ground to favor public operation, so that you had a public-power bill passed by a Republican Congress, vetoed by President Coolidge in 1926, another vetoed by President Hoover in 1931.

This legislation entrusted to a regional agent of the Federal Government twenty years ago flood control, navigation improvement, and power generation in the Tennessee Valley area. Today, there are thirty major dams in the Tennessee River system, and half a dozen major interconnected steam plants.

[7] From a report on the Tennessee Valley Authority presented to President Eisenhower on October 8, 1953, by Governor Frank G. Clement of Tennessee. *Reporter.* 9:28-32. December 8, 1953. Reprinted by permission.

This system provides security from floods to thousands of acres of land in the Tennessee Valley and reduces flood hazards to an additional 6 million acres of productive land along the Mississippi River. Flood savings average about $11 million a year, with more than half these benefits outside the Tennessee Valley.

This same multi-purpose system provides a broad waterway 650 miles long, which is a part of the 8,000-mile inland waterway system and has as truly become a vital part of the economic life of the region. Where traffic in 1933 amounted to 33 million ton-miles—most of this was sand and gravel which moved short distances—traffic now is nearing one billion ton-miles annually and includes oil and gasoline, automobiles, coal, steel and iron products, fertilizers, corn, and wheat. Shippers using the Tennessee are now saving more than $10 million a year in transportation charges. . . .

The assignment for developing the broad use of power recognized its close relationship with flood control and navigation, and was in keeping with the traditional American concepts that the electric business, whoever owns and operates it, is a public business. Today, the region has a hydroelectric generating capacity of 3,291,435 kilowatts and 1,836,550 kilowatts of steam power. Use of electricity has grown from 1.5 billion kilowatt-hours in 1933 to 27 billion kilowatt-hours in 1953 and is increasing at an accelerating rate.

TVA set out to generate and transmit electric power, but the people of the Valley "put it into the distribution field." Every state in the area passed a law authorizing municipalities and rural areas to vote on concentrating with TVA for electricity. And they were not long in taking advantage of their opportunity. In rapid succession they voted the private power companies out of the Valley.

In no other major area of the country do the local people do more of the job of distributing electricity than in the Tennessee Valley area. Ninety-seven municipalities, fifty-one rural cooperatives, and two local private companies own and are operating and paying for distribution facilities to deliver TVA power to some five million people.

The individual communities decided, usually by vote, to do the job this way, and local merchants, bankers, farmers, doctors, lawyers, and teachers serve on the boards that direct the affairs of the local systems and see that maximum local benefits are attained.

These local systems are developing widespread use of electricity at low rates, the goal stated by Congress in the TVA Act. In 1933 only 3 per cent of the farms in the region had electric service. Today, 90 per cent of the farms have electricity and many areas are practically 100 per cent electrified. *The average domestic consumer in the region uses approximately twice as much electricity as the average for the entire nation, and pays only half as much per kilowatt-hour.*

When the nation was plunged into World War II, the revitalized Tennessee Valley proved a bulwark of national defense. The tremendous electric energy potential of the Tennessee Valley was a major factor in choosing a site for the first atomic plant in the United States and in the success of this country in the atom-bomb race. Though perhaps the most dramatic contribution of TVA to the war effort, this was by no means the only one.

The region's agriculture, its productivity restored by the TVA fertilizer and test demonstration program, poured out record quantities of food and fiber to help meet the needs of the nation at war. TVA chemical facilities at Muscle Shoals produced 60 per cent of the munitions-grade elemental phosphorus used by the armed forces and its electric-furnace research aided industry in producing the other 40 per cent. Throughout the Valley the hundreds of private industrial plants whose machinery was turned by TVA power added their part to the production of defense materials.

TVA's contribution to the tremendous power demands of the atomic-energy program did not end with the war. Today, a major portion of the expanding TVA power-generating facilities are earmarked to supply the AEC with 25 billion kilowatt-hours per year for the new atomic-energy plant at Paducah, Kentucky, and for expanded plant at Oak Ridge, Tennessee.

More than half of TVA's total output of electrical energy is used regularly in the production of materials essential to the national defense.

By 1956, TVA will be supplying 25 billion kilowatt-hours a year to the Atomic Energy Commission's plants at Oak Ridge, Tennessee, and Paducah, Kentucky. *It is nearly double the amount of hydroelectric power than can be produced on the TVA system in a year of average rainfall.* This power must obviously be provided by new steam-power plants.

While there is some hydroelectric potential still to be developed in the region, it is small in relation to the growing power needs.

Earnings from the sale of TVA power have averaged, for the past twenty years, better than a 4 per cent return on the investment devoted to power operations. This is considerably more than the cost of money to the Federal Government and sufficient for TVA to keep well ahead of the congressional requirement that all funds appropriated for power operations be paid back to the United States Treasury within forty years after the facilities are placed in service. In addition, power operations have provided more than $200 million for investment in transmission lines and other power assets which are the property of the Federal Government.

Mr. President, perhaps you are preparing to ask me how so sound, so solvent, so beneficial, so high-purposed, so esteemed an institution as TVA could incur the general, all-out and bitter attack of the private power industry—or at least that of its leading spokesmen? The advertisement writers of the National Association of Electric Companies are making much of the private power companies as *private enterprise.* That claim is less than a half-truth. What they are, in fact, is private *monopoly.* And they are monopolies of public business.

Since the beginning, we have in this country considered the power business, whoever owns and operates it, a public business. The idea is as indigenous as cornbread. Private corporations engaged in the electric business enjoy *privileges* granted by the public. They use the public streets and roads as right of way for poles, lines, and underground circuits; they are permitted to exercise the sovereign right of eminent domain to secure land and right of way for their plants and facilities; they are granted exclusive marketing rights over defined areas, or at a defined level; laws are passed to assure them a reasonable level of earnings.

Why have they been, why are they now given these unusual privileges by the public? First, electricity is not just another "commercial product," as they would have us believe, to be placed on the commodity market at the highest price it will bring. Electricity is energy, a basic necessity of community and national life, an absolute requirement for minimum national strength and security. Every community is entitled to an adequate supply at reasonable rates.

Because of its vital nature and because of the great capital investment necessary to generate and distribute it, we have not subjected generation and sale of electricity to the conditions of free competition—the spur, the tonic, the police, the very life blood of private enterprise. In our great belief in private enterprise, in our faith in its wholesomeness for society, we have granted private corporations monopolistic protection, under public regulation. That this compromise was questionable is evidenced by the fact that there have been publicly owned electric systems since the beginning. Indeed, in 1882, the more or less accepted date of birth of the industry, there were four publicly owned electric systems.

Public regulation of these private electric power monopolies in this country before TVA was not notably successful. It was this very ineffectuality that nurtured public operation over the years, even though, because it was done at the municipal level and in small generating units, it became increasingly uneconomical. It was, if you please, this very lack of success that eventually converted practical-minded members of Congress to the public management of power in the Tennessee Valley—not for the sake of public power, mind you, Mr. President—but for the cause of *private enterprise!* . . .

The truth is that private enterprise cannot thrive—yea, cannot *live,* without the whip of competition.

And that, if you please, is just what Congress intended when it put TVA into the power business, and that is just what TVA is today.

Private corporations generate and sell four fifths of all electric power in this country today. And roughly, as a ratio between private and public operation that is, perhaps, sound. The TVA does not aim at the socialization of the power industry in this country. God forbid! Such an eventuality would defeat the very purpose for which it was given stewardship over the Valley's electricity. It could no longer operate as both the bundle of fodder and the bull whip to spur on the ineptly harnessed team of Private Enterprise and Public Monopoly.

The private-utility spokesmen have been crying for some years about the unfairness of TVA competition. But they don't present any figures to show who or how many were put out of business. The private power industry doesn't appear to be anemic today nor is it weak of voice—not judging by the report that it spent $20 million last year promotionally, most of which was devoted to its fight against TVA. To be exact in the matter, TVA, of course, does not compete with private power companies in their respective franchise-protected territories. The competition is merely by example and often it has been by inducement. . . .

Mr. President, I say let the private power industry yell its head off at TVA—the situation is wholesome for both of them. But don't take their rage too seriously.

To take the TVA to be a pattern for nationalizing the power industry is to wholly misunderstand its significance. It is peculiar to the Tennessee Valley, where through intelligent conservation it has brought to us great economies in the use of our natural resources. It performs no service that has not been long performed through some one or another of the existing departments of the Federal Government. It merely decentralizes these services to the regional level and places them in one agency.

It is a blessing of our windfall that we have low power rates; nevertheless, we pay our way. It is no inconsiderable national blessing that the TVA windfall provides this country with something of an electric power stockpile against emergencies. And finally, this unique congressional mandate of which I have already spoken was to inspire the private power industry, not destroy it—the fact that the national average electric rates have been reduced by 60 per cent since TVA came into existence is evidence that it has and is carrying out that mandate.

III. THE TIDELANDS

EDITOR'S INTRODUCTION

The Submerged Lands Act, which became law on May 22, 1953, was passed "to confirm and establish the titles of the states to lands beneath navigable waters within state boundaries and to the natural resources within such lands and waters, to provide for the use and control of said lands and resources, and to confirm the jurisdiction and control of said lands and resources, and to confirm the jurisdiction and control of the United States over the natural resources of the seabed of the continental shelf seaward of state boundaries." For purposes of the act, natural resources include "oil, gas, and all other minerals, and fish, shrimp, oysters, clams, crabs, lobsters, sponges, kelp, and other marine animal and plant life but does not include water power, or the use of water for the production of power." The seaward boundary of each state is defined as "a line three geographical miles distant from its coast line or, in the case of the Great Lakes, to the international boundary" (Public Law 31, 83d Congress, 1st session, H.R. 4198, 67 Stat 29).

Thus the Republican party fulfilled its campaign promise to give away—or to give back—to the states the tidelands properties, the most important aspect of which were the oil rights. In the controversy which centered around this issue, the major arguments dealt with the legal ownership of the submerged lands (as defined, chiefly, by court decisions), and with the estimated value of these properties and the tax revenues involved. The first three articles which follow discuss the historical basis of ownership of the marginal sea and the events leading up to the 1953 act, while the fourth and fifth pertain to the dollar value of the properties going to the states. In the final selection, the possible effects of the Submerged Lands Act on the conduct of our international affairs are reviewed.

TIDELANDS OIL [1]

All through United States history, until recent years, everybody who lived on the ocean assumed that when the tide went out, all the land from high tide down to low tide, and from there on out, including rocks, gravel, seaweed, mussels, lobsters, oyster beds, and everything else (including oil) belonged to the state, or could be taken only with permission of the state, as far out as one could see, and at least to the "three-mile limit," which was as far as a cannon-shot would go in the days when men began to make rules about such things.

Even people in the Federal Government took this for granted. When the government wanted to build a lighthouse, or the Army wanted to build a dock, or for any other of many reasons the Federal Government wanted some land beyond the level of high tide, it got it from the state government.

But all this was upset in 1947 by the Supreme Court. It said that the Federal Government has "paramount rights and full dominion and power over" such lands (except for "inland waters"). True, it refused to say that the Federal Government *owned* such undersea land. But the decision came to the same thing. It effectively dispossessed the state government of California, and three years later the state governments of Texas and Louisiana, from all their established and historic rights in coastal subsea land, without any recompense and with the effect of making anyone who leased from the state automatically a trespasser on the Federal Government's "paramount rights" and "full dominion."

This decision had something of the effect of an earthquake on the whole practicing profession of state and municipal lawyers. It pulled the rug from under a large part of the business of their state and city employers. So widespread were the implications that the winning government lawyers, as has happened before with similar astonishing

[1] From article by Harold M. Fleming, a New York newspaperman and freelance writer. *U.S.A., the Magazine of American Affairs.* 1:99-105. June 1952. Reprinted by permission.

Supreme Court opinions, hastened to say that the Federal Government would not push its new powers to the limits apparently granted. The Attorney General said that only the coastal sea bottoms where oil or something "important to national defense" is found would be claimed by the Federal Government.

However, the city and state lawyers soon thought they saw much wider meanings and conclusions to be drawn from what the Supreme Court's six-to-two majority said. (Justice Black wrote it.)...

On the surface it looked as though all that the Supreme Court in its wisdom had done had been to take away from the seacoast states a three-mile belt of water looking out to sea. But it soon turned out to be far more complicated than that. The lawyers for California presently pointed out to the court that there do not exist any clear-cut meanings for such terms as three-mile belt, inland waters, bays, ports, and harbors. And they listed 104 segments or areas along California's 1,100-mile coast whose status required definition. Did they belong to the state or were they under Federal "dominion"?

Second thoughts were even more worrisome. On a second reading the lawyers discovered that the Court had said California had a "qualified" ownership of lands under inland navigable waters such as rivers, harbors, and even tidelands down to the low-water mark. This sounded bad; at law the word "qualified" is not much different from what the layman means by "questionable."

It sounded even worse when the lawyers recollected an ancient Anglo-Saxon tradition, which long went for a legal precedent. It ran to the effect that it was because the king owned the "marginal sea" that he owned the bays and navigable waters—not vice versa. He owned the bays, lakes and river bottoms as "arms of the sea." And so (reasoned the lawyers) if the Supreme Court took the "marginal sea" away from the states (and gave it in effect to the United States Department of the Interior) then it might take away the bays and navigable waters also when it saw fit.

And this, essentially, is why the state authorities became so instantly alarmed. . . .

It also explains why the Massachusetts General Court approved a resolution in favor of having Congress pass a law to renounce the Federal Government's claims; why forty-five states have publicly supported such legislation; and why such a quit-claim law . . . [was] publicly favored by the American Title Association, the American Association of Port Authorities, the Council of State Governments, the National Conference of Mayors, the National Reclamation Association, the National Water Conservation Association, the (State) Governors' Conference, the National Institute of Municipal Law Officers, and the American Bar Association.

In a sense it was a "bunch of oil men" who jarred down this ceiling of broken plaster about the heads of the state government people.

The so-called and somewhat misnamed "tidelands" controversy has now been raging since 1937. If any single group started it, it was a team of oil drillers putting down a well on the California coast near Huntington about 1927. By accident they discovered that they could drill a crooked well, and make it go in the direction they wanted. This was the beginning of "directional drilling." The direction they chose was from the land out under the sea. There they ran into the (supposed) title of the state of California.

In the early thirties, as such drilling increased, a number of speculators conceived the idea of getting tickets to join the party, in the form of leases, not from California, but from the United States Department of the Interior.

Mr. Ickes was the head of Interior in those days. His earlier answers to these applications are now a sad joke to state and municipal lawyers. He replied to one of them on December 22, 1933, that "it has been distinctly settled that title to the shore and lands under water inures to the state. . . . Title to the soil under the ocean within the three-mile limit is in the State of California."

Still the applicants and their lawyers pushed. If they could only succeed, they might get leases on ground already proved up by someone operating on a State of California lease. And finally Mr. Ickes changed his mind.

Mr. Ickes twice had resolutions introduced in Congress to the effect that the marginal seas belonged under Federal control. Both were soundly defeated. And there the matter rested until 1945, when the Attorney General sued the State of California for trespass, and as above indicated, won a resounding victory in the Supreme Court.

Meanwhile, the following things had happened.

As the Court test loomed, Congress passed a "quit-claim" bill to specify that marginal seas did not belong to the Federal Government. The President vetoed it on the ground that Congress should wait on the Court's decision. Subsequent efforts continued in succeeding years but were blocked, chiefly in the Senate, by Administration pressure.

The President in 1945 proclaimed:

Having concern for the urgency of conserving and prudently utilizing its natural resources, the government . . . regards the natural resources of the subsoil and sea bed of the continental shelf . . . as appertaining to the United States, subject to its jurisdiction and control, and [they] are hereby placed under the jurisdiction and control of the Secretary of the Interior for administrative purposes.

In 1947, the Texas legislature voted to extend the territory of Texas to the edge of the continental shelf. In 1950, the Supreme Court followed up its 1947 decision against California with similar decisions against Louisiana and Texas. This time the Court extended the Federal Government's "paramount rights" and "full dominion" to the edge of the continental shelf. The Court enjoined the states and their lessees from any further mining or drilling in these submerged offshore lands without authorization from the United States. . . .

The layman may wonder how the majority of the Supreme Court reached a position so astonishing even to the lawyers.

The Supreme Court majority admitted that in the past the Court had

used language strong enough to indicate that [it] then believed that states . . . owned soils under all navigable water within their territorial jurisdiction, whether inland or not.

But, said the majority,

The crucial question is not merely who owns the bare legal title to the lands . . . the United States here asserts rights in two capacities transcending those of a mere property owner. In one . . . it asserts the right and responsibility to exercise whatever power and dominion are necessary to protect this country. . . . The government also appears in its capacity as a member of the family of nations . . . responsible for conducting . . . relations with other nations. . . .

The Supreme Court majority also overruled a plea of "estoppel." The California lawyers argued that since government officials had acted for generations as though the states owned these lands, the Federal Government could no longer lay claim to them. "Estoppel" is the time-honored legal principle that you cannot agree one way for a long time and then change your mind and come into court and argue another way. But the Supreme Court majority ruled that the government was not to be deprived of its interests in this case "by the ordinary court rules designed particularly for private disputes over individually owned pieces of property."

What constitutional lawyers . . . [found] of greatest importance in this decision . . . [was] not that the Court majority denied state ownership in marginal seas, and thus upset the always delicate adjustment of power between the Federal and state governments. That was bad enough—for the states. Of far broader meaning than that, however, was the majority's exposition of what has come to be called the doctrine of "inherent sovereignty." A layman might call this a blurring of the difference between sovereignty—which the government has over everything—and property. It suggests that the United States, for reasons of national defense and foreign policy, might at will, and without compensation, convert its sovereignty into "full dominion" over every river, farm, mine and factory of the nation—and by this doctrine make an end-run around Article V of the Bill of Rights, which says that private property shall not "be taken for public use without just compensation."

It seems fairly obvious that the main drive behind the tidelands issue is oil. [Former] Secretary of the Interior Oscar Chapman has said:

> It is only through management of these lands by the central government that we can hope to attain integrated conservation policies with respect to oil and gas development, and the coordination of development policies with the needs of national defense and commerce. . . .

The proof of the pudding is in the eating, and the proof of management is in production. The Federal Government's record for producing the goods is a dismal one.

Federally owned lands total over 400 million acres. They come to about a quarter of the total area of the continental United States. Most of them are in the West, where they come to more than half the area of some states.

But the amount of oil they have produced is negligible. They include, particularly in the 180 million acres owned and operated by the Bureau of Land Management, some areas covering the nation's greatest potential petroleum production. But of the 40,000-odd oil wells being drilled annually, only about 2 per cent have in recent years been drilled on government land. A considerably smaller per cent of the "wild cat" or exploration wells are drilled on Federal land. During World War II only about 3 per cent of the nation's production of oil came from government-owned lands.

As for government revenues from this small amount of drilling and production, it is barely enough to cover the cost of the bureaus which regulate it.

During World War II the Army spent $150 million on the so-called "Canol" project in Canada and Alaska. It produced a million barrels of oil, and quit. That was (not counting the value of time of Army Engineers) something around $150 per barrel. Civilians do it today for around $2.65 per barrel.

It may be laboring a point, but the following conclusions seem to apply.

(1) The country seems to face the choice of more Federal power and less oil, or the reverse—more oil and less Federal power.

(2) The allergy of the Constitutional Fathers to centralized government seems still to have a sound economic basis.

(3) If Congress . . . [gave] up its battle against the President and the Supreme Court majority to keep the nation's offshore oil resources out of the hands of Interior, it . . . [might] prove, in the eyes of later historians, to have sold the nation's political birthright for a mess of petroleum —without getting the petroleum.

WHO OWNS THE OIL UNDER THE SEA? [2]

Geologists have estimated that the known petroleum resources lying under the coastal waters of California, Louisiana, and Texas are worth about $40 billion. Starting about twenty years ago, when oil began to be produced in appreciable quantity off California, the governments of these states began to lease offshore lands to petroleum prospectors as a matter of course, since it was universally acknowledged that the individual states had complete control over their inland waters. Meanwhile, offshore oil has become a rich source of revenue to the three state treasuries, and the major oil companies having offshore leases prefer to continue doing business with the easy-going state governments rather than with the Federal Government. Even so ferocious a protector of the national domain as the late Secretary of the Interior Harold L. Ickes took it for granted that this oil lay properly within state jurisdiction and outside Federal authority.

Late in the 1930's, however, it was suggested to Ickes that a large portion of the offshore lands containing oil might lie outside navigable inland waters and therefore outside state jurisdiction. He and the then Attorney General brought

[2] From article by Alan Barth, editorial writer on the Washington *Post*. *Reporter.* 7:25-7. November 11, 1952.

suit, first in a Federal district court, then directly in the
Supreme Court, to determine what authority the United
States could properly assert in this area.

The very term "tidelands" is a complete misnomer as it
is generally applied. "Tidelands," properly speaking, means
the strip of land that is submerged when the tide is in and
exposed when it is out. This land is not involved in any
way in the contest between the states and the Federal Government. The states have indisputable title to the tidelands
adjacent to their respective seacoasts. The Federal Government does not dispute this title.

Neither does it raise the slightest question as to state
ownership of "inland waters"—the rivers, lakes, bays, and
ocean areas within coastal indentations — as distinguished
from the open sea. The President, the Attorney General, the
Secretary of the Interior, and every other interested Federal
official has categorically and redundantly renounced any
claim whatever to such areas. Moreover, a long line of
Supreme Court decisions going back for more than a century
has held uniformly that inland waters and tidelands belong
to the states. The point was unequivocally restated in the
Court's recent ruling on the subject.

The correct term to apply to the controversial area is
"marginal sea." This constitutes the area lying seaward of
the low-tide mark out to the traditional three-mile limit of
national sovereignty. It is this area—and this area alone—
concerning which the Supreme Court declared, first in the
California case in 1947 and again in the Louisiana and
Texas cases in 1950, that the states had no title and that the
United States possessed paramount rights.

Beyond the marginal sea and the three-mile limit, the
edge of the North American continent extends for varying
distances into the Atlantic, the Pacific, and the Gulf of Mexico—at some places for a distance of 250 miles. This indefinite area of submerged land is known as the "continental
shelf." President Truman issued a proclamation in 1945
asserting to the rest of the world that the natural resources
of the sub-soil and sea bed of the continental shelf off the

United States coast "appertain to the United States, and are subject to its jurisdiction and control." No foreign government has challenged this assertion. But some of the coastal states of the Union have claimed ownership of the continental shelf—that is to say, extension of their state boundaries—to various distances seaward, for twenty-seven miles in the case of Louisiana and more in that of Texas.

It is important to understand just what the Supreme Court said in addition to just what area it dealt with in its marginal-sea decisions. The crux of the Federal Government's suit against California was a distinction between tidelands or inland waters on the one hand and the marginal sea on the other. Acknowledging that state ownership of tidelands and inland waters had long been established, the Federal Government contended that this did not include the open ocean and that title to the marginal sea, therefore, had never been determined. The Supreme Court accepted this distinction, declaring explicitly that the question of the marginal sea was brought before it in this case for the first time.

As for the marginal sea, the Court said not only that California had no title now but that California had never had any title. Ownership of land beneath ocean waters (as distinguished from inland waters) is a matter of international law. The Court did not say that title was vested in the United States. It said simply this:

> Now that the question is here, we decide for the reasons we have stated that California is not the owner of the three-mile belt along its coast, and that the Federal Government, rather than the state, has paramount right in and power over that belt, an incident to which is full dominion over the resources of the soil under that water area, including oil.

The Court came to this conclusion in large measure on the ground that "not only has acquisition, as it were, of the three-mile belt been accomplished by the national government, but protection and control of it has been and is a function of national external sovereignty." It would seem to be the view of the Court, in brief, that national sovereignty and dominion over any part of the open ocean are inseparable.

California and Louisiana never possessed national sovereignty and therefore could never have possessed the marginal sea, let alone any further portion of the continental shelf. The same can be said of all the other states of the Union with the exceptions of Texas and Florida. For nine years before entering the Union by compact, Texas was an independent and sovereign republic, undoubtedly possessing the rights of sovereignty over the submerged lands at least to a distance of three leagues from its shore. By the Supreme Court's logic, however, Texas inevitably relinquished these rights when it relinquished sovereignty, transferring them to the sovereign United States.

Whatever the merits or demerits of this reasoning may be—and three Justices dissented from the majority view—the Supreme Court's opinion stands as an unquestionably authoritative determination of the Federal-state controversy. Indeed, the Supreme Court was expressly created under the Constitution to resolve just this kind of controversy. The lawsuit has been won by the Federal Government; and so far as the law is concerned, there can be no reasonable doubt as to the Federal Government's supremacy over the marginal sea.

But California, Louisiana, and Texas have sought to accomplish through the legislative and executive branches of the government what they could not accomplish through its judicial branch. On two occasions they have persuaded Congress, though not the President, to quitclaim, or renounce title to, the marginal sea—and, incidentally, to portions of the rest of the continental shelf for good measure. This legislation has been expressed in terms of giving back to the states their rightful possessions, or confirming titles that a misguided Supreme Court has slightly clouded. But what it amounts to, of course, is an outright gift by the Federal Government of land that the Supreme Court says belongs to the country as a whole.

The pretense of the legislation passed by [the Eighty-second] Congress . . . [early in 1952]—that it aims merely "to Confirm and Establish" state titles—is at best disingenuous. If, as the Supreme Court has declared, the states never had any title to the marginal sea, confirmation is an impossibility.

Of course, Congress can confirm state titles to inland waters. But there is not much point in confirming what is unquestioned. The motive that led the President to veto the "tidelands oil" bill . . . [in May 1952] was that it did not confine itself to tidelands but aimed to stake out a state claim to a much wider area. In his veto message, Mr. Truman said:

> If the Congress wishes to enact legislation confirming the states in the ownership of what is already theirs—that is, the lands and resources under navigable inland waters and the tidelands—I shall, of course, be glad to approve it. But such legislation is completely unnecessary, and bears no relation whatever to the question of what should be done with lands which the states do not now own—that is, the lands under the open sea.

A BASIC NATIONAL ISSUE [3]

Two labels have done much to confuse and obscure the real issues over the ownership of the submerged lands. One is "Tidelands" and the other is "Oil."

"Tidelands" technically means the beach or shore between high and low water marks. This, everyone agrees, belongs to the states. The area which has been fought over is the seabed extending three miles seaward from the low watermark. This is the so-called historical boundary of the states, with the exception that Texas and the west coast of Florida have owned historically such an area for a distance of ten and a half miles seaward.

[3] From "Tidelands . . . A Basic National Issue," article by Hall Hammond, Associate Judge of the Maryland Court of Appeals, formerly Attorney General of Maryland and Chairman of the Submerged Lands Committee of the National Association of Attorneys General. Baltimore. 46:11+. May 1953. Reprinted by permission.

Oil, and the wealth associated with it, and the "oil-rich tidelands," have been headlined in the press and dramatized in the halls of Congress by proponents of Federal control, until many believe that oil is all that is involved.

It is true that oil precipitated the controversy because an applicant for an oil lease caused Secretary Ickes to change a century-and-a-half-old belief and policy, and for the first time assert Federal ownership of the area. But the real fight is over the place of the states in our constitutional system— *it is the fight of centralization of power in the executive branch of the Federal Government against local self-government.*

There is an alarming overtone in a new legal concept, expressed by the Supreme Court for the first time in the case in which it held that the United States had "paramount rights" over the disputed area.

The senators who fought to keep the area from being restored to the states argue that since the Supreme Court has declared that the United States has paramount rights, Congress will be delivering untold wealth in oil into the hands of capricious and probably corrupt state officers in three coastal states, so that oil for national defense would be dissipated and that national resources, belonging to all of the people, will be delivered to the people of three states. The position of the defenders of the rights of the states, I shall explain shortly, but first, the real facts should be set forth as to the area involved, as well as the amount of oil and the value thereof.

The so-called continental shelf, which at points extends as much as one hundred miles from shore, contains approximately 1.5 billion acres. The area within the historic boundaries of the states contains a total of only 17 million acres. It is almost universally agreed that the United States has exclusive paramount rights which Congress will spell out over all of the continental shelf, except that area within the original boundaries of the states.

Dr. Ralph Miller, Chief of the Fuel Branch of the United States Geological Survey of the Department of Interior, estimates that of the oil in the whole continental shelf, only 17 per cent would go to the states under the proposed legislation to restore their rights, while 83 per cent would go to the United States. The same source estimates that the proven oil reserves now existing off-shore in California, Texas and Louisiana are about 260 million barrels. This is approximately a thirty-two-day supply of oil for the entire nation. The royalties which could be expected to accrue over a period of twenty-five or thirty years would be approximately $30 million to the three state governments. This is the fabulous wealth and the vital oil reserves which have been shouted about and used to mislead in the controversy. . . .

By 52 decisions of the Supreme Court, by 244 state and Federal Court decisions, 49 opinions of the Attorneys General of the United States, and 31 of the Solicitors to the Department of Commerce, it was as established as anything could be, that the states owned the land under the sea for a distance of at least three miles from the shore. . . .

In 1946, the Supreme Court in the case of *United States* v. *California* . . . (followed as a matter of course by similar decisions against Louisiana and Texas), overthrew these titles . . . and held that the United States had paramount rights. Before the decision, the Congress of the United States had passed a bill saying that the Federal Government had no interest in the area and that the states had always owned it, but President Truman vetoed it. . . .

The Supreme Court decision has been said to be wrong by almost all legal students and scholars who have considered it. There have been some forty-five law review articles on the subject and forty-two of them have been very critical of the decision. . . .

Every state has submerged assets. Several years ago, Maryland leased drilling rights to one of the large oil companies and received royalties of $20,000 a year for several years for acreage off its ocean coast in Worcester County. The proponents of Federal control now agree that the Chesapeake Bay is an inland water and therefore, not owned by the Federal Government. They do this, however, only on the

basis that it is an "historic exception" because under the
rules of international law, its headlands are far enough apart
to make it a part of the open sea. *It would be a very easy
jump for some future power-hungry Federal-ownership bureaucrats to claim that the Chesapeake Bay is owned by the
Federal Government.*

Robert Moses, who has done so much to develop the port
of New York and its surrounding areas, feels strongly that
title to hundreds of millions of dollars of improvements in
New York, particularly on Long Island, require the passage
of legislation validating the claims of the states to areas
seaward of their dry boundaries. The Great Lakes States
own iron ore of tremendous value under the water of the
Lakes. Minnesota has received more in royalties from iron
ore than Texas has from oil. Maine gets $14 million annu-
ally from its marine resources, mostly kelp. Alabama has
7 million acres of submerged lands under mineral leases,
including leases of sand and gravel.

Federal proponents now claim only land under the ocean
and the gulf, denying any intention of claiming under the
Great Lakes or other inland waters. In hearings before congressional committees, however, up to very recently, the
Federal bureaucrats would not agree that the Great Lakes,
for example, were inland waters, because they said things of
great value might be found under them which the Federal
Government would want.

The legal possibility of the extension of the doctrine of
the California case as to marginal seas to the inland waters
is very great. A part of the decision of the Supreme Court
in the California case was that it would not extend the so-
called inland waters rule—and the Department of Justice
challenged the validity of that rule in this case—under which
the states owned the beds under lakes, rivers or harbors to
the open seas.

The Court, it seems unquestioned, made a legal and historic mistake because the doctrine of the ownership by the
sovereign of submerged lands began with lands under the
seas and extended inland, because the inland waters were

arms or tributaries of the seas. In other words, the extending was from the sea inward, and not from inland waters outward. . . .

The most alarming and potentially far-reaching doctrine of the California case was that the United States controlled the historic boundaries of the states seaward, because it had paramount rights; that is, that the necessities of defense or the making of war enable it to take what it needs without compensation. As far back as 1939, the Departments of Interior, Justice, and Navy, argued in a brief that:

the United States may exercise paramount rights in the soil in navigable waters of the United States to provide for the common defense or to provide and maintain a Navy without the payment of compensation to the states of their representatives.

Witnesses for this point of view before the congressional committees have said that the Federal Government could go, for example, into Mobile Bay or the Alabama River and take oil without the payment of compensation, and that they could, for example, take oysters from the Chesapeake Bay without compensation, if needed to feed the Navy. The dissenting Justices in the California case, the American Bar Association, and the National Association of Attorneys General, have all agreed that if national responsibility can enable the government to take oil without compensation from the marginal seas, it can enable it to take coal from Pennsylvania, or iron ore from Minnesota, or timber in Maryland, or even every mine or factory in the nation, under the same theory.

Congress has consistently recognized that the states were right in this fight but every time it has passed a bill, it has been vetoed. One bill passed by the House in 1948 was supported by 90 per cent of the members without a single vote against it from thirty-five of the states, and with no majority against it from any state.

Apparently, the long fight of the states is about to be successful, since President Eisenhower has expressed an intention to sign the legislation which President Truman always vetoed, and Congress undoubtedly will pass the final legislation. Both the House and Senate recently approved the new tidelands bill (H.R. 4198) giving the states clear title to submerged lands out to their historic boundaries. [As indicated in the introduction to this section, the Submerged Lands Act became law on May 22, 1953—Ed.]

OIL UNDER THE SEA [4]

In its attempts to turn over much of the national wealth to private industry, the Eisenhower Administration has had to resort to some fancy footwork. This has been particularly true in the case of the oil and chemical industries, where such cute variations as the "sell-away" and the "lease-away" have been developed.

The first and biggest giveaway, of course, was that of offshore oil, which was accomplished by the Holland bill . . . [which passed as the Submerged Lands Act and became law on May 22, 1953]. There was no need to be too clever here; the Republicans had promised this gift to the oil industry before they were elected. In one stroke the Holland bill allowed between ten and fifty billion dollars' worth of oil and mineral lands to pass out of the Federal domain. These lands consist of submerged offshore oil fields out to the historical three-mile limit, mainly off Texas, Louisiana, Florida, and California—along Texas and Florida the lands run out ten and a half miles. The Holland bill simply turns these submerged lands over to the states. The result is twofold: the people of the forty-five states who can't prospect for oil under an adjoining ocean get nothing, and the oil companies, which will do the actual exploiting, will operate outside Federal jurisdiction and will have only the weak regulatory powers of the state governments to contend with. Indeed, prospects are good that the companies will end up with actual ownership of the submerged oil fields.

[4] From article in *Nation*. 179:280. October 2, 1954. Reprinted by permission.

Oil and gas royalties which normally accrue to the Federal Government from oil produced on public lands are set at 12.5 per cent; sulphur royalties at 5 per cent. Senator James Murray has estimated that on the basis of the most conservative estimate of the value of the oil the Federal Government has lost more than $6 billion in revenue.

The significance of the loss was dramatized by Senator Hill's unsuccessful effort to retain the tidelands oil for the Federal Government and to devote the income to Federal aid to education. . . . Hill urged that the billions involved be distributed to the states under a formula based partly on population and partly on need: the allotment would be greater to states unable to provide adequate education from their own resources.

Despite the billions the United States spends on education, this is a still a country where overcrowded classrooms are the rule in cities and the one-room school is still standard in rural areas. How the Hill plan could have helped this situation is shown in the following table. The first column shows estimated expenditures on public education for 1953-54, including local, state, and Federal funds, as compiled by the National Education Association. The second shows how much additional money each state could expect to get over the years from the Hill plan. The table represents a sampling only; every state in the union would have benefited from the plan.

	1953-54 Expenditures (Est.)	Hill Amendment Revenue
Alabama	$87,071,000	$358,000,000
Arkansas	53,000,000	232,000,000
California	747,000,000	404,000,000
Florida	144,600,000	185,000,000
Georgia	140,500,000	365,000,000
Louisiana	126,999,000	273,000,000
Mississippi	48,920,000	284,000,000
New Mexico	41,428,000	72,000,000
New York	777,000,000	470,000,000
So. Carolina	121,000,000	263,000,000
Wyoming	18,600,000	21,000,000

An ironic postscript has been added to this story. When the tidelands bill was first introduced, conservationists and other public-land defenders set $10 billion as the minimum value of the properties that would be given away. Oil-industry experts said it would not amount to more than half a billion. A month ago *Barron's*, the business weekly . . ., in a report on the first explorations being made on these submerged lands by the oil companies, said, "Beneath this part of the continental shelf there is estimated to be some ten *billion* barrels of crude, or nearly one third of total estimated on-shore reserves." At current prices this amounts to nearly $30 billion.

VALUE OF TIDELANDS OIL [5]

Opening up the tidelands for oil drilling isn't going to make any millionaires or change the economics of the oil industry overnight. It will be a slow, costly business. And it will demand a tremendous investment.

That's the conclusion that the National Petroleum Council has reached after a year's intensive study. NPC is a permanent industry advisory committee that works with the Interior Department. Hence, its report is about as close as you'll get to an official industry position on the subject.

During the long fight over whether the tidelands belonged to the Federal Government or the states, President Truman estimated that $80 billion worth of oil lay beneath the submerged lands off California, Texas, and Louisiana. That may be true, says NPC. But it adds that the final settlement—giving the states title to all the oil lands out to their traditional seaward boundaries—won't start any drilling boom.

Costs will be too great. It is going to take a staggering amount of time and money to get the tidelands oil into anybody's gathering tanks. For a long time, the operation may

[5] From "Tidelands Oil Won't Produce Any Fortunes Overnight," article in *Business Week.* p77-8. June 27, 1953. Reprinted by special permission from *Business Week*, a McGraw-Hill publication.

cost more than it yields in revenue. The tidelands offer virtually no opportunity to the independent wildcatter with his limited funds. Hence, even if the states are ready to lease the tidelands, the industry will be slow to move in.

On the average, it will cost more than twice as much to develop producing wells in the offshore areas as on dry land, the council found. In many cases, a well may cost five times that of an equivalent one on land. Take a look at some actual figures.

Installations and equipment to drill, say, ten wells in sixty feet of water in the Gulf of Mexico from six platforms would cost more than $5.7 million. The same number of wells on dry land would take only $1 million.

Actual drilling cost estimates run between two and three times more than on land. The tab for drilling five vertical and five directional holes to depths ranging from 10,000 feet to 12,000 feet, for instance, would total $8.2 million, compared with $3.2 million on land.

This ominous report came from a committee set up by the National Petroleum Council . . . to survey the potential availability of petroleum in the tidelands.

The group, made up of experts on tidelands exploration and drilling, did not even hazard a guess on the ultimate amount of oil and natural gas that may be discovered and produced. But on two points it was positive: Years will pass before any sizable production can be expected from the Gulf of Mexico, and prospects for adding greatly to production off the shore of California are not too bright.

In fact, the committee estimated that after five more years of active exploration and drilling in the Gulf, the most the nation can expect to produce is between 70,000 barrels and 100,000 barrels a day. How puny this production is shows up when you compare it with the 6.25 million barrels the United States coughs up today, and the national daily consumption of more than 7 million barrels.

The industry experts believe that an added production of 100,000 barrels a day can be obtained in the Pacific Ocean in the same period, but only if California amends its drilling law to permit well drilling from platforms off the shore. Under existing law, all drilling starts from land and is slanted out under the water.

Obviously, there will be no stampede into the submerged lands such as followed the inland discoveries in Texas, Oklahoma, and other states—even on the part of the big oil companies. In fact, it may be some time before actual new operations are started.

President Eisenhower's signing of the tidelands act, restoring full title to the offshore lands to the adjacent states out to historic boundaries, is only a first step. Congress still must set up Federal control and leasing machinery for the underwater area in the continental shelf—an as yet undefined extension of the United States coast. The big question the states and the Federal Government are still arguing: What part of the shelf belongs to the states and what part to the Federal? And the argument may take several years.

Moreover, the threat of litigation to test the validity of the tidelands bill passed by Congress this year still hangs over their heads. Officials of several of the largest leaseholding companies have indicated that they will not risk any more big capital until such litigation is decided, or until it's clear that none will be filed.

In their report, the experts agree that the opening of the continental shelf to drilling operations may eventually add great quantities of oil and gas to the nation's reserves. But for the present at least, development beyond the traditional boundaries of the states will be strictly limited.

TIDELANDS LEGISLATION AND THE CONDUCT OF FOREIGN AFFAIRS [6]

I appear at the request of the Committee to testify on questions concerning the international relations of the United States which have arisen in the course of the hearings of

[6] Statement by Jack B. Tate, Deputy Legal Adviser of the Department of State, made on March 3, 1953, before the Committee on Interior and Insular Affairs of the House of Representatives. Reprinted from *United States Department of State Bulletin.* 28:486-7. March 30, 1953.

this Committee on control and development of mineral resources in submerged lands off the coasts of the United States.

I should make it clear at the outset that the Department is not charged with responsibility concerning the issue of Federal versus state ownership or control. It is concerned solely with the effect which the legislation might have upon the conduct of foreign affairs.

I shall summarize first the historic position of the United States with respect to the question of control which a coastal state may exercise in the waters adjacent to its coasts. I shall review briefly the policy reasons which lead this government to follow and maintain this position. And I shall finally examine the points which appear to involve a possible conflict with our traditional position in this field of foreign relations.

The position of the United States with respect to the control which a coastal state may exercise involves three areas: inland waters, territorial waters, and high seas.

The relevance of considerations concerning inland waters is this. The belt of territorial waters is measured from the coast. On the land portion of the coast, the line from which territorial waters are measured is the low water mark of the tide. Since bodies of waters such as bays, gulfs, rivers, etc., also open on the coast, it is necessary in such cases to use a fictional line from which to measure territorial waters. The position of the United States is that the waters of bays and estuaries less than ten miles wide (or which are, at the first point above such openings, less than ten miles), are inland waters of the United States, and the territorial limit is measured from a straight line drawn across these openings. A strait, or channel, or sound which leads to an inland body of water is dealt with on the same basis as bays. But the waters of a strait which connect two seas having the character of high seas are not inland waters.

It is an essential feature of inland waters that they are assimilated for all intents and purposes to the land territory of the coastal state, and foreign vessels may not claim in such waters a right of innocent passage. Foreign vessels may, however, claim a right of innocent passage through straits connecting high seas. . . .

As early as 1793, this government had to face the question of the breadth of territorial waters. At that time Jefferson, while reserving a final decision, took the position that the United States should consider territorial waters "as restrained for the present to the distance of one sea league or three geographical miles" from the seashore. This position has never been changed. The United States supported the three-mile limit at the 1930 Hague Conference for the Codification of International Law. And in the last few years, this government has on a number of occasions reaffirmed this position and protested the claims of other states to limits broader than three miles, including the claim of the Soviet Union to twelve miles.

In adhering to the three-mile limit, the United States does not preclude itself, of course, from taking all steps necessary to prevent or repel threats to its national security.

Preventive measures such as the establishment of Defensive Sea Areas for national defense purposes have been established in the past, and some are still in effect under current legislation. . . .

Nor does the United States preclude itself from exercising jurisdiction on the high seas, beyond the three-mile limit, for certain purposes. A good example is the legislation, enacted as early as 1790, providing for the exercise of jurisdiction within twelve miles from the coast for purposes of customs control. . . .

The claim made by the United States in the Presidential Proclamation of September 28, 1945, to jurisdiction and control of the national resources of the subsoil and seabed of the continental shelf off its coast is one more example of the compatibility between the United States position on the three-mile limit and the protection of its interests. This government did not claim sovereignty, or an extension of its boundaries beyond the limit of three miles of territorial waters. Indeed it specified in the proclamation that the character as high seas of the waters above the continental shelf and the right to their free and unimpeded navigation are in no way affected.

I now turn to the reasons for the adoption and maintenance of this position. The purpose of this government has been, and still is, to give effect to its traditional policy of freedom of the seas. Such freedom is essential to its national interests. It is a time honored concept of defense that the greater the freedom and range of its warships and aircraft, the better protected are its security interests. Likewise, the maintenance of free lanes and air routes is vital to the success of its shipping and air transport. And it is becoming evident that its fishing interest depends in large part upon fishing resources in seas adjacent to foreign states.

The maintenance of the traditional position of the United States is vital at a time when a number of foreign states show a tendency unilaterally to break down the principle of freedom of the seas by attempted extensions of sovereignty over high seas. A change of the traditional position of this government would be seized upon by other states as justification for broad and extravagant claims over adjacent seas. This is precisely what happened when this government issued its proclamation of 1945 regarding jurisdiction and control over resources of the continental shelf. It precipitated a chain reaction of claims, going beyond the terms of the United States proclamation, including claims to sovereignty extending as much as two hundred miles from shore.

The Department is concerned with such provisions of proposed legislation as would recognize or permit the extension of the seaward boundaries of certain states beyond the three-mile limit. In international relations, the territorial claims of the states and of the nation are indivisible. The claims of the states cannot exceed those of the nation. If the nation should recognize the extension of the boundaries of any state beyond the three-mile limit, its identification with the broader claim would force abandonment of its traditional position. At the same time it would renounce grounds of protest against claims of foreign states to greater breadths of territorial waters. This is without reference to the question as to whether the states should be permitted to exploit the resources of the continental shelf beyond state boundaries.

The Department believes that the grant by the Federal Government of rights to explore and develop the mineral resources of the continental shelf off the coasts of the United States can be achieved within the framework of its traditional international position.

IV. PUBLIC LANDS

EDITOR'S INTRODUCTION

The issue of state versus Federal ownership of natural resources, which arose initially in the case of the tidelands properties, soon developed into a debate on public land policy generally. President Eisenhower's reference to a partnership of states, local governments, private citizens, and the Federal Government as being "effective . . . in the sound use of public lands," as well as the congressional decision giving the coastal states rights to the submerged lands, led to predictions that the Federal Government might consider granting to the states some of the federally owned lands.

The statements by Senator Hunt and Representative Rodino, which follow the introductory article, "All Public Lands Going to States?" illustrate the effect of the tidelands issue on congressional thinking regarding public lands. Judge Sawyer then analyzes the uses for which the public domain and the national forests are held, concluding that these functions are most adequately fulfilled under public ownership. Representative D'Ewart's reply argues for increased state control of the public domain; it is his belief that "public ownership should be utilized only when other controls prove to be inadequate or when damage from possible abuse would be too irreparable to risk."

The position of the National Chamber of Commerce on the issue of public lands is set forth in "The Way Back to Land Freedom," and Wallace Stegner in the selection which follows sees the issue not as a struggle between state and Federal governments, but "between the public interest and the powerful private interests that for years have tried to corral the West's land, water, timber, and water power." The status of private forestry, and its progress during the past decade, are described in the final article.

ALL PUBLIC LANDS GOING TO STATES? [1]

An idea is stirring through the West that Congress might be induced to turn over to the states the vast Federal Government holdings in public lands.

It was out of public land, federally owned, that twenty-nine states of the Union were carved. In the West, even today, the Federal Government owns more than half of all the land, ranging from 35 per cent in Washington to nearly 85 per cent in Nevada. This ownership involves immense stands of timber, vast tracts of grazing land, valuable water rights for power and irrigation projects, areas now held as undeveloped reserves that may be rich in metals and oil. In addition, there are great stretches of mountains and deserts with little value except as scenery.

When President Eisenhower and Congress became interested in turning offshore lands over to coast states, the West pricked up its ears. Here seemed to be a political opening that might be exploited while the mood of the country was changed. President Eisenhower added to the West's interest when he remarked at a news conference that he favored giving to states some of the public lands within their historic boundaries. As a result, bills of various kinds are taking shape to go to Congress.

But transferring public lands to states or private owners turns out to be no simple problem. Not everyone in the West favors the shift. Some groups see more benefit from Federal ownership than from state or private ownership. Others would be satisfied to have the government change the rules regulating the use of public lands. Still others simply want the Federal Government to pay state and local taxes on its real estate.

Chief targets in proposals to transfer public lands are the Bureau of Land Management in the Interior Department and the Forest Service in the Department of Agriculture. These agencies are the country's biggest landlords. They

[1] Article in *United States News & World Report.* 34:25-7. March 27, 1953. Reprinted from *United States News & World Report,* an independent weekly news magazine on national and international affairs published at Washington, D.C. Copyright 1953, United States News Publishing Corporation.

control 180 million acres each. On these lands graze about 46 per cent of all western livestock. From them come about 22 per cent of all timber cut in the West. They also form a large part of the western watershed.

Timber interests are in the forefront of advocates who favor transferring public lands to the states. At the least, they want the Forest Service rules changed to permit greater private operations in the national forests. They argue that the Federal Government holds 72 per cent of the timber stands in the West, but these stands produce only a fraction of the lumber.

Lumbermen argue further that more cutting would improve the condition of the national forests. The contention is that the Forest Service lets trees stand too long, thereby choking younger growth and preventing proper cultivation of timber resources. The Forest Service counters that national forests must be preserved from excessive cutting and that no more timber should be cut than is grown. Present policy is aimed, they say, at preventing the stripping of forests that has occurred outside of the national preserves.

Grazing lands, managed chiefly by the Bureau of Land Management but in part by the Forest Service, also are eyed by some private livestock interests. There is considerable pressure to sell grazing lands that are available for year-round use to private operators. But not all livestock growers favor this. The majority of small growers of sheep and cattle seem to be content with Federal ownership, but many would like the grazing rules changed. They would like to be allowed to run more stock and to be sure that their grazing rights will not be changed by regulation. One sheep man, for example, is irked by a Forest Service order to cut to half the herd he had been grazing on forest lands for the last fifteen years.

Most livestock growers seem to regard use of Federal grazing lands as a relatively cheap service. The public domain can be grazed by private operators at moderate rentals. One Nevada rancher explained: "Do you think that cattlemen could afford to buy 85 per cent of Nevada's lands and pay taxes on that?"

Mining interests, too, are generally satisfied with Federal ownership of public lands that might contain minerals. They can obtain mineral rights on these lands from the government, paying royalties on any discoveries. Few private concerns could afford to carry the millions of acres in the public domain that might contain minerals. They would prefer more lenient tax allowances that recognize the expense and risk of mineral exploration. . . .

Most of the public lands are lands that nobody wanted as the West was settled, and hence remain under Federal ownership. And it has been Federal policy since 1902 to conserve and develop what remained. Furthermore, most of the land is put to what is called "multiple use," such as grazing, hunting and fishing, watershed control and stream development, requiring public supervision. There is still powerful support for leaving this management in Federal hands. . . .

The 11.6 million acres in the national parks also are likely to stay under Federal ownership. These are recreational areas and wild-life preserves that are viewed as national playgrounds. However, there is increasing pressure to have the parks make some payments to states and counties. Park Service officials are reported to favor this policy.

The outcome of the present stirring in the West over public lands thus is likely to leave most of those lands under Federal ownership. But the Federal Government appears very likely to be obliged to make larger payments to states on these lands, and a few of the more valuable tracts may be sold.

IMPLICATIONS OF TIDELANDS FOR OTHER PUBLIC LANDS [2]

As a culmination of three decisions of the Supreme Court involving oil under submerged seaward lands bordering

[2] Statement made on March 30, 1953 (before passage of the Submerged Lands Act, which became law on May 22, 1953), by Representative Peter W. Rodino, Jr. (Democrat, New Jersey). Text from *Congressional Digest*, an independent monthly magazine (not a government publication) featuring controversies in Congress pro and con. *Congressional Digest.* 32:296-7. December 1953. Reprinted by permission.

California, Texas, and Louisiana there is a concerted effort by those states, and by other states fearful of possible exclusion from a future opportunity to obtain control of natural resources, to obtain a quitclaim or transfer these oil resources.

If this effort succeeds, it merely will be the opening wedge to a drive to accomplish the same type of transfer of all public lands, mineral resources, national forests, land-grant railroad rights-of-way, and other reserves of the Federal Government. [The effort was successful. See Editor's Introduction to Section III above, "The Tidelands."] These tremendous reserves and resources are found largely in eleven western states where, it is admitted, they create serious problems of tax revenues and apportionment of responsibility between the Federal and respective state governments. Percentagewise, the Federal holdings of the total land area in these eleven states are said to be as follows: Arizona, 73 per cent; California, 46 per cent; Colorado, 38 per cent; Idaho, 64 per cent; Montana, 35 per cent; Nevada, 87 per cent; New Mexico, 44 per cent; Oregon, 53 per cent; Utah, 72 per cent; Washington, 35 per cent; and Wyoming, 51 per cent. . . . Lands in the states admitted earlier are practically all privately owned and subject to taxation. It is this inequality, of course, which excites much of the criticism in the West. . . .

It is said that no public lands can longer be identified in Illinois, Indiana, Iowa, Missouri, and Ohio. Small areas may remain in Alabama, Kansas, Louisiana, Michigan, Mississippi, Oklahoma, and Wisconsin in widely scattered and located tracts. Thus, the bulk of the nation's remaining reserved natural resources exist in the eleven western states, noted earlier, and in the Territory of Alaska, and it is this bulk which is always involved in any effort to transfer public domain to any given state.

No one can deny that Congress has the constitutional power to divest itself of these natural resources by transferring them to the states, for the Constitution specifically says, in Article IV, section 3, clause 2, that the Congress shall have power to dispose of the territory or other property belonging to the United States. This power was clearly recognized in the first tidelands case *United States* v. *California* (1947)—wherein Mr. Justice Black, speaking for the majority, stated:

We cannot and do not assume that Congress, which has constitutional control over governmental property, will execute its powers in such a way as to bring about injustices to states, their subdivisions, or persons acting pursuant to their permission.

Thus, even the decision of the Supreme Court, holding that California, and later Louisiana and Texas, did not own the marginal belt along their coast, and deciding that the Federal Government rather than the states has paramount rights in and power over that belt, an incident to which is full dominion of the resources underneath the water area, including oil, cannot preclude legislation by Congress under the above noted constitutional provision disposing of that property.

Acknowledging this constitutional power of Congress to dispose of the property of the United States does not establish, necessarily, the merits of disposition. It has been said that the reserved oil deposits beneath the marginal seas constitute a huge public trust held by the Federal Government in the interest of all the people of the United States. They are enormously valuable, and there is no more impelling reason why they should be given to the bordering states than that other reserved natural resources should be given to the respective states in which they are located. Historically, it is interesting to note, the revenues from the sale of lands in the ceded Northwest Territory were used to liquidate the national debts incurred in the American Revolution.

As stated earlier, the transfer of these lands will merely be the opening wedge of a drive to accomplish other transfers. Of great importance are the national forests, the reserved power sites, the public grazing lands, and the mineral reserves. Capitulation to quitclaimism, whereby the United States would be persuaded to renounce blindly to states sovereignty over millions of acres of seaward lands, would lead to the ultimate destruction of all Federal conservation, public land, and public power policies and would result in the exploitation and waste of the remaining natural resources of the nation. This would not be in the best interests of the nation.

TIDELANDS OIL RIGHTS AND SUBSURFACE MINERAL RIGHTS [3]

From my point of view the underlying principles and conditions with reference to the tidelands and subsurface rights in public lands in the western states, ownership and administration of which are now under the jurisdiction of the United States, are identical. Fifty-three per cent of the land area of Wyoming is federally controlled, and Wyoming, therefore, as to matters which to my way of thinking are purely local, is under the jurisdiction of a dual administration. . . . I am thoroughly convinced that the mineral rights underlying federally owned lands can be administered more directly and more profitably by local government than by the Department of the Interior—and I am not one who, generally speaking, is critical of the Department of the Interior.

I have never been able to understand the theory or reasoning behind the retention by the Federal Government of the ownership of mineral rights in the western states, when that theory is not and never has been applied to states not designated as public-land states. We of the western states are as rightfully entitled to the revenues produced from minerals under public lands in our states as are the states in coastal areas involved in the so-called tidelands issue.

If these mineral rights are given to my state, income from them would make Wyoming self-supporting to a far

[3] Statement made on February 9, 1953, by Senator Lester C. Hunt (Democrat, Wyoming), following his introduction on February 6, 1953, of S.807, a bill providing for granting to the states, with certain exceptions, the mineral rights in public lands belonging to the Federal Government. (This bill did not pass.) Text from *Congressional Digest*, an independent monthly magazine (not a government publication) featuring controversies in Congress pro and con. *Congressional Digest*. 32:293+. December 1953. Reprinted by permission.

greater extent, and thus lessen, if not entirely eliminate, a need for grants-in-aid programs.

In the year 1952 alone, the Federal Government was enriched to the extent of approximately $18 million by mineral production in Wyoming, and since 1920 my state from such production has turned over to the Federal Government $153,250,000, which, I may say, rightfully belongs to the people of the state of Wyoming.

My bill does not provide for the transfer of surface rights to the state, in that I feel the surface rights—the extensive grazing areas, the huge wildlife population, the national parks, the wildlife preserves, and the national forests, including wonderful fishing areas—bring such recreation, pleasure, and profit to all the people of the United States that administration should remain with the Federal Government for the benefit of all the people.

FEDERAL CONTROL OF THE PUBLIC LANDS SHOULD BE RETAINED [4]

In the course of its history the United States has been the owner of nearly three fourths of the land within its borders. By one route or another, two thirds of its holdings have gone into other, and for the most part private, ownership. Most of this title change took place more than forty years ago. Then there began reacquisition by the Federal authority in an amount that now stands at, in round figures, 53 million acres. Roughly half of this acreage has been acquired for national forest purposes. There are, however, several categories of lands in Federal ownership that have been reserved for special uses. Among them are the national parks, the national monuments, wildlife refuges, military

[4] From address by Robert W. Sawyer, of Bend, Oregon, newspaper editor and publisher, former county court judge, and member of many conservation groups, at a forum dealing with the question "The Public Lands—Who Should Control Them?" The forum was part of the Mid-Century Conference on Resources for the Future, sponsored by Resources for the Future, Inc., and held in Washington, D.C., in December 1953. Address summarized in *The Nation Looks at Its Future*, a report of the Conference. Resources for the Future, Inc. 1145 19th St. N.W. Washington, D.C. 1954. p361-3. Reprinted by permission.

reservations, Atomic Energy Commission lands, power lines and irrigation project rights-of-way, reservoir floors. Here, ownership and control go hand in hand, and with these lands therefore we are not immediately concerned.

Of the public lands we are here considering, the national forests are the cream, and the so-called unreserved public domain the skimmed remainder of Uncle Sam's land estate. The public domain—some 180 million acres—is virtually all in the eleven western states. So, too, is by far the greater part of the national forests in which are the lands that were first withdrawn to create the watershed and forest reserves. Together these two acreages include approximately 80 per cent of the nation's total public land. Ninety per cent of all lands in the present Federal total have never been in private ownership.

Each of these classes of land—the public domain and the national forests—is an area of multiple uses, five in all. On each there is grazing; from each timber is taken. Grazing is the more important use on the public domain; the tree supply is more important in the forests. Two other uses of these lands are for recreation and wildlife habitat. Finally, there is the use that transcends everything else—maintenance of water supply.

These five uses may be divided into two classes—profit uses and service uses. The profit uses include a rather wide spread of commercial ventures using public domain land, but chiefly they are engaged in by private operators, both big and little, whose use of the public domain is in association with use of their own lands for ranch or mill. They, or some of the more vocal of their number, would like control of these lands. That is why the question before us is posed. Shall they control these public lands or shall the control be in the hands of the people of the nation through their Federal Government? There is only one possible answer: These public lands should be controlled by their owners—the people of the United States.

The profit motive is the cornerstone of our great American private enterprise system. With that motive there can be no quarrel. Throughout that system, however, there are restraints and regulations enforced for the common good, and here on the public lands where there are service uses vital to our national well-being the profit uses must be subordinated. That subordination calls for public rather than private control.

At one time there was no control on the public domain lands other than that exercised by the man with the water hole and the Winchester. The profit use only prevailed. No attention was paid to the service uses of the land. Under these conditions, the one-time sea of grass that covered the western range ceased to be. There was overgrazing. There was erosion. There was a quick runoff of precipitation instead of ground storage. Streams dried up. Brush and noxious weeds succeeded grass.

This abuse of range led, finally, in 1934 to the passage of the Taylor Grazing Act. Though a considerable acreage of the public domain was not covered, 140 million acres were reserved for regulation. However, appropriations have never been adequate for effective administration. Just when they had reached a point where the bare essentials of range management could be effectively applied, they were cut back so as to render the administration—the owner, if you please—impotent in control of the land. Today, the users have the upper hand. Private profit use rather than public service use predominates.

In the national forests, public control of the profit use has been far better established and maintained. But efforts have constantly been made—measures are pending even now —to limit the public control of the forest range. What the Forest Service seeks in its management of the profit uses of the forests in its care is sustained yield of the forage on the range and of the timber capital.

In operating these public lands and making them or their products available for profit uses, their Federal managers under the authority of congressional legislation, have set up regulations, uniform throughout all areas. This would not be possible were the control otherwise situated, when the profit motive would, of necessity, dictate the operations. The sum of this is that there should be public control of the profit use and since there is no profit in the service uses there must be public control.

Concerning these service uses: Recreation and wildlife are unimportant to the profit use, if not actually obnoxious. The managers of the public lands are as aware as are the owners of private lands of the dangers involved in keeping lands open for the free use and enjoyment of the general public. They know it will not pay direct dollars and cents dividends. But they and all the rest of us know that in our country service uses of this kind are something the public has a right to expect—something that in the long run will pay dividends worth much more than dollars. These service uses such as hunting, fishing, hiking, camping, winter sports, unimpaired natural scenery, and the general recreation opportunities which are a part of the multiple use values of the public lands require, for their preservation, control of these lands by the Federal authority.

And now I come to the most important use of all—the use of the public lands for the protection, management, development, and maintenance of water supplies. Water is basic to our food supply. It is an essential in industry. Without water we perish. And in wide areas of the United States the water supply comes entirely or largely from the public lands.

There exists in many of our mountains a delicate balance between soil, vegetation, and water. We cannot log, graze, or build roads on some steep hillsides without seriously interfering with this delicate balance. Other areas may tolerate the removal of forest crops if carefully done, while still larger expanses present no difficulties in the harvesting of all forest crops.

Nature, as weather, plays a high part in the annual water drama, but man can have an influence, too, and whether that influence is for the good or for the bad, depends on how he has managed the public lands. Proper management or use of land should be the highest goal to be sought, but it is not a profit use. Its earnings are chiefly for the downstream water users, the local public of that watershed. The control, then, of these public lands where the waters rise should be in the hands of the people and managed by their Federal agencies.

For our public lands as a whole I urge that, since in unregulated profit use there is bound to be disregard of service use values, there must be regulation; and the control of all should be in the hands of the owners—the people of the United States to whom the service uses are next to invaluable in the matter of wildlife and recreation, and supremely invaluable in the matter of water.

MORE STATE AND LOCAL PARTICIPATION NEEDED IN PUBLIC LAND MANAGEMENT [5]

I can agree with Judge Sawyer on his objectives, but I do not altogether agree with him on the road by which we should reach those objectives.

Let us take a look at the present control of these public lands we are discussing which, if we exclude the national parks and monuments, national wildlife refuges, Federal water projects, military reservations, wilderness areas, and that part of the national forests that is not primarily used for grazing, comprise some 310 million acres of Federal-owned land generally classified as timber and grass land.

First, there are some five thousand laws, and regulations beyond number, controlling their use and management. Second, the areas are now under the direction of three departments divided into eight or more bureaus and agencies each with its own personnel, each under different law and regulation, each charging different fees for use, and each with its own objectives—often in conflict with another agency or government. To add to the difficulty of management, the areas under different bureaus and agencies are often intermingled. Lastly, the head offices of these agencies in Washington,

[5] Summary of reply to the preceding statement of Judge Sawyer by Representative Wesley A. D'Ewart (Republican, Montana). *The Nation Looks at Its Resources.* Resources for the Future, Inc. 1145 19th St. N.W. Washington, D.C. 1954. p363-5. Reprinted by permission.

D.C., are hundreds of miles away from the lands which they administer. All this makes for a complex landlord-manager-tenant relationship in which you and I are the landlords, the bureaus are the managers, and the local users are the tenants. Certainly, no one will argue that such a situation of present control and management is in the best public interest.

What should be our objectives? I think they can be briefly stated: conservation—that is, wise use without waste; development of the great natural resources that are found on and under the surface of these public lands; revitalization of our renewable resources; maintenance of adequate reserves of nonrenewable resources until substitutes are found. In the development and use of these resources, we should encourage private enterprise; solicit the cooperation of local government and institutions; go forward with Federal action only when the public interest cannot otherwise be served; maintain at all times the rights of the individuals and the integrity of the states; and avoid monopoly.

Fundamentally, I believe that whenever possible, private responsibility for protection of land is best for this country. It places the burden of protection on the beneficiaries; it allows development without government expense; it brings an economic factor of cost versus benefit into the picture; it gives political stability and soundness to the nation by respecting the rights of individuals as partners in national welfare. Let no one think that I advocate policies contrary to good conservation practice; I feel that self-interest is a conservation force; that policing power can be effective under local governments; and that public ownership should be utilized only when other controls prove to be inadequate or when damage from possible abuse would be too irreparable to risk.

It was no accident that enemies of the American system put the elimination of private property as their first objective. The trends of recent years do not represent what is best for the United States. We must reverse them insofar as they fail to contribute positively to the benefit of this nation.

President Eisenhower, in a message to Congress on July 31, 1953, set forth a program for the control, development, and wise use of these public lands and the resources on and under them. He said:

Our basic problem is to carry forward the tradition of conservation, improvement, and wise use and development of our land and water resources—a policy initiated fifty years ago under the leadership of President Theodore Roosevelt. To do this within the framework of a sound fiscal policy and in the light of defense needs will require the maximum cooperation among the states and local communities, farmers, businessmen, and other private citizens, and the Federal Government. . . . It will require the revitalization of renewable resources by users who should be entitled to reasonable assurances in connection with authorized uses. It will require adherence to sound principles for the financing and the sharing of the cost of multipurpose land and water resource development. It will require improved Federal organization to accomplish a more logical division of responsibilities among the various Federal agencies in order that resource development programs may be carried on with the greatest efficiency and the least duplication. It will require comprehensive river-basin planning with the cooperation of state and local interests. . . . Public lands should be made available for their best use under conditions that promote stability for communities and individuals and encourage full development of the resources involved.

Here you have a program in our best tradition, one that will require the maximum cooperation of all of us as individuals, state and local communities, and the Federal Government. It is not planned that the Federal Government shall carry on alone. Clear guidelines must be enacted setting forth its proper functions. It is hoped that through the new Hoover Commission and through the Commission on Intergovernmental Relations many of the objectives set forth in the President's message can be worked out.

My state of Montana has long recognized its responsibilities in the control of its resources and has set up under state law a Grass Conservation Commission, a Forestry Board, an Oil and Gas Conservation Commission, a Park Service, and a Water Conservation Board. It has provided for irrigation districts, weed control districts, soil conservation districts, state grazing districts, and has taken other steps to assure the wise use, development, and control of our great natural resources. Montana's record in resource management and development completely refutes the belief in some circles that the states are somehow subject to baneful influences and are not competent to manage their own affairs.

In the same circles, there has been a growing belief that the people cannot be trusted. Yet one of the greatest forces for conservation is the self-interest of the individual in protection of his property. I hope that we will use this force to the fullest possible degree.

The people of the fourteen western states, where half of the surface is federally controlled, think that there are those among their citizens who are to be trusted to cooperate wisely in the management of these areas in the best public interest. They recognize that the special areas I have already mentioned as being set apart are great national assets and that their benefits reach far beyond the state in which they happen to be located. These should remain in Federal control and the responsibilities of the Secretary in charge should not be impaired. However, public-spirited citizens wish for a greater measure of local recognition in the development and use of these areas and they feel they could make a material contribution to their use and development. In addition, there are certain parts of the public domain . . . whose use and development are primarily local. These areas should be re-examined to see if some of them cannot be better managed by the states and in some instances placed on the tax rolls. . . .

In the control, management, and use of these public lands we must never lose sight of the fact that our greatest asset is a strong, upright, free citizenry. Such a citizenry can be developed, not by bureaucratic control, but by use of its capabilities through encouragement in the wise use of our great natural resources.

A WAY BACK TO LAND FREEDOM [6]

There are few things more fundamental to the well-being of American society than the freedom of land ownership. It

[6] From speech by Laurence F. Lee, then president of the United States Chamber of Commerce, before the National Lumber Manufacturers Association. *American Forests.* 58:15+. February 1953. Reprinted by permission.

is a cornerstone of our economy. Most of our forebears came here in search of human rights that had been denied them in the old world. They sought religious freedom and political freedom, but they also sought land freedom. They founded this country on the solid premise of strength and abundance through the genius of free men applied to the land and its resources.

Unlike some of our present-day reactionaries who appear to think in terms of land ownership as it existed in the feudal ages, our forebears recognized that property rights are also human rights. They knew that tyranny has its roots in land that is held and controlled by a few political figures.

The classic case of tyranny today is Communist Russia. The Soviet Union is the world's largest landlord. All of the land is owned or at least controlled by the central government. When the Communists plowed under the freedom of land ownership, they also buried the other human rights.

The United States Government is on the way to becoming the world's second largest landlord. The trend has been in that direction for at least the last two decades.

This trend is [a] complete reversal of the principle behind our Homestead Acts in the nineteenth century. The Homestead Acts made government the agent of the people to open the undeveloped West and give every man a chance to earn land for himself through his own skill and hard work.

In the nineteenth century, our government diffused land ownership. In the twentieth century, it has been taking the land back. That is not progress. That is sheer reaction.

As of today, the numerous land-administration bureaus of the Federal Government own 24 per cent of all the land in the United States. In the last twenty years, the government has increased its acreage in the eleven western states from 33 per cent to 54 per cent.

No one seems to know exactly how much acreage is held by the Federal Government, but we do know it exceeds 455 million acres, exclusive of Indian reservations and of Federal lands in Alaska and other territories. Even the Federal bureaus themselves do not know how much they own.

Representative Russell V. Mack (Republican) of Washington told the House of Representatives . . . that more than forty Federal agencies are involved. Sixteen different agencies control federally-owned timberlands. And no two have the same ideas on how the Federal property should be managed. . . .

Most of our fellow citizens are probably not aware of . . . [these facts] or at least not aware of the danger inherent in Federal ownership of land. . . .

Do they know what the lack of land freedom does to their pocketbooks? To the sovereignty of their states? To community government? To the elementary and secondary schools and state colleges and universities? These are the things they ought to know. The facts of the case have a vital appeal, for they are directly related to the family budget.

Do the American people know that the Federal Government does not pay taxes to the states in which its holdings are located? Do they know that the Federal land empire deprives the states of taxes on 24 per cent of the entire United States? Do they know that everyone must pay for the high cost of having these lands administered by the Federal Government?

In some instances, the Federal Government pays the state a portion of the gross receipts in lieu of taxes. But these payments are not uniform as to percentage among the various bureaus, and they are far from uniform as to amount from year to year. Payments are made only when revenue is derived. When no timber is sold or minerals mined, no payments are made. With rare exceptions, the states and local governments receive less in the long run under any system of Federal ownership than they would receive if the lands were properly held and operated by private, taxpaying owners.

How many people are aware that the more land the Federal Government owns, the easier it is for still more land to be acquired through the process that you call "trading stumps for stumpage?"

By this process, the timberland owner is invited to exchange his cutover lands—which means his future productive capacity—for trees—not land—of the Federal Government. This type of exchange enlarges the Federal holdings and reduces the productive land in private ownership.

The timberland owner is precluded from acquiring land of his own on which to practice good forestry, and broadly speaking, people are interested in good forestry and conservation practices.

Now it is true, of course, that there might be no particular harm in Federal ownership of undeveloped lands—such as those of the public domain—so long as there was a program for disposal of such lands. But in this era of Federal acquisition, we find the Federal Government has designs on 35 million acres of timberland to enlarge the national forests, and . . . the Department of the Interior has [recently] withdrawn from disposal 112,000 acres of public domain forest lands in northern Arkansas. . . .

I wish to quote the National . . . [Chamber of Commerce] position on this vital national issue:

The Congress should undertake an examination, by departments, of the Federal real estate inventory to the end that all property, which, in the public interest, is best adapted to private ownership, be offered for sale as soon as possible and thus be placed on the tax rolls and in productive use by private enterprise.

In order to provide more accurate data on Federal lands not recommended for private ownership, it is further recommended that studies be undertaken of the problems involved in conservation and use of such lands, including their relation to lands in state and private ownership, such studies to be conducted in the several states by joint boards made up of representatives of Federal, state and private land ownership.

There is no doubt of a latent public interest in this problem, but it is imperative that the state-by-state and bureau-by-bureau study be made as soon as possible. The longer the task is delayed, the more acute the problem will become, and the more impossible it will be to solve.

In proposing such a study, we do not advocate that all land held by the Federal Government should be turned over to private ownership. National parks, for example, and the research areas, forested lands necessary for watershed protection, certain military reservations and similar areas probably are best adapted to Federal ownership. Acquisition, retention or disposal—in every case—should depend on what is best for the public interest.

It seems to me that the forest products industries should assume leadership in drafting and supporting appropriate legislation for study of the land ownership problem. . . .

Such a group, in drafting corrective legislation, might give consideration to these points:

First, as to registration of Federal lands. A description of all lands under Federal ownership should be registered with the Department of Interior and recorded statistically to show the annual rate of acreage increase or decrease. This would end the present confusion as to the exact extent of Federal land ownership and give us an annual picture of what is happening.

Second, ask the Congress to set up joint boards representing Federal, state and private land ownership to provide more accurate data on Federal lands and to establish a criterion on which to base the type of ownership.

Third, ask the Congress to undertake an examination of Federal lands to see what property is best suited for private ownership to the end that it be offered for sale to the public, under proper safeguards, as soon as possible and thus be placed on tax rolls and in productive use by private enterprise.

And, fourth, during the period of such registration and examination to suspend all acquisition, through trades or otherwise, except those for military use. . . .

The trend toward government ownership of land has jeopardized the sovereignty of states; it has added to the tax burden; it has jeopardized the revenue for elementary and secondary schools, for state colleges and universities, and for community purposes. It is potentially a menace to all private enterprise from which the financial and defensive vigor of our country is derived.

PUBLIC LANDS AND ITCHING FINGERS [7]

There is a brand of states-rightism that is more western than southern, more Republican than Democratic, and based not on history or sentiment but on natural resources of enormous value. And yet the real struggle is not between states and the Federal Government but between the public interest and the powerful and persistent private interests that for years have tried to corral the West's land, water, timber, and water power.

More than the resources themselves are involved. Almost as important are the intangible assets: the protection of watersheds and the regulation of stream flow and the control of silt; the conservation of the "biotic layer" of the topsoil upon which all life depends; hunting, fishing, recreation, and the propagation and protection of wild life; and the international security that is based on having adequate oil reserves.

If Federal ownership and management of resources in the public interest is "creeping socialism," then socialism has been creeping for a long time. The first major exception to the policy of complete disposal implicit in the Homestead Act of 1862 was the reservation of Yellowstone National Park in 1872, with the purpose of preserving it from private exploitation. The national forests date back to the Forest Reserve Act of 1891; most of the reservations were established by Presidents Harrison, Cleveland, McKinley, and Theodore Roosevelt, who were fought every step of the way by patriotic Americans eager to "develop" timber resources.

The system of leasing public lands for mineral and oil extraction began with the Mineral Leasing Act of 1920, amended several times since but not altered in its basic assumption that the lands involved were going to remain in government hands. The same lease system was applied to the range land by the Taylor Grazing Act of 1934. That

[7] From "One-Fourth of a Nation—Public Lands and Itching Fingers," article by Wallace Stegner, author and student of public land problems. *Reporter*. 8:25-9. May 12, 1953. Reprinted by permission.

Act, to all intents and purposes, ended the period of disposal and settled us in the policy of local management under Federal ownership.

Of the principal acts of legislation that brought the change about, only the Taylor Grazing Act was passed under the New Deal, and even that was the product of almost sixty years of agitation. It was fathered by a Democratic congressman from Colorado, Edward Thomas Taylor, who had fought Federal authority over the public lands for years. And while it was on its way through Congress, Washington was visited by the same persuasive force that had converted Representative Taylor: Wind from the Dust Bowl blew across half the nation to sift dust on the streets of the capital itself.

By and large, all Federal assumptions of responsibility for management have come as emergency rescue operations. The Civilian Conservation Corps, the Soil Conservation Service, and other innovations of the 1930's found their work and their justification in a mined-out and eroded public domain. A large part of the Federal land purchases in the past twenty years has been of overgrazed, eroded, or otherwise submarginal land that had either to be retired from use or become desert.

One after another, as its resources began to disappear before exploiters careless of the future, the nation rescued what it could of its wilderness areas, its timber, its water, its essential minerals, and its range. In more than fifty years, the only real breaks in the development of this policy have been two Republican Administrations, Taft's and Hoover's. There are many who think the third, and most dangerous, may be the Administration of Dwight D. Eisenhower. . . .

Conceivably, concerted attacks at this time could overturn the whole policy of Federal management. They are likely, however, to be only partly successful, to whittle out of government hands the most productive elements now federally owned or to remove the controls that now prevent great profits by land and power companies and speculators.

The grazing lands, including those within the national forests, are in danger; public power is in danger; the 160-acre water limitation within reclamation projects is in danger. . . . Maybe these riches will ultimately be restored, but they will probably return gutted, eroded, and mined out, when they are of no further use to private owners. Then the nation can try to restore them.

It may be taken as gospel that the strongest antagonism to government ownership and management will be found among those who would profit most from their elimination. Whatever the diversionary tactics and political smoke screens, the issue is public interest vs. private profit. If stockmen or land owners grow wrathful about Federal absentee landlordism and call for the "return" of Federal lands to state tax rolls (where they never have been), they do so because a powerful local group can dominate a state government more easily than it can a Federal bureau.

Consider the tactics of the stockmen's attempted raid on the Federal lands in 1946-1947. Following up [the late] Senator [Pat] McCarran's [Democrat, Nevada] emasculation of the Taylor Grazing Act and working through friendly western members of Congress such as former Senator Edward V. Robertson [Republican, Wyoming] and former Representative Frank A. Barrett [Republican] of Wyoming (now a Senator), the National Livestock Association proposed that all Taylor Grazing District lands be turned over to private ownership. As a second step it wanted reclassification of grazing lands within the national forests, parks, and monuments. Once reclassified, these would be turned over with the Taylor lands to the stockmen. One of the prime objectives was to gobble the Jackson Hole National Monument. Another was to escape government supervision over grazing and the limitations on the animal units per month that could be run on government land.

They might have got the grazing lands alone, for the Grazing Districts were almost helpless and the lands themselves enlist no one's sentiment, as the parks and forests do. But in extending the grab to the parks and forests the stockmen challenged conservationists and vacationers, and these people rose up in such numbers that Representative Barrett's House Committee on Public Lands, which had set out to hold hearings throughout the West, crept home protesting the innocence of its intentions. So violent was the purely western opposition to the stockmen's proposals that the chief of the Forest Service thought the threat could not arise again for years to come.

But before 1953 was a fortnight old, the Livestock Association was making public noises about "the return of the Federal lands to the tax rolls of the states." Characteristically, it neglected to say that the states on being admitted to the Union gave up any claim to these lands or that in acquiring them the states would saddle themselves with conservation and management costs, expose the lands to overgrazing and erosion again, and reduce the amount of Federal aid for roads and other improvements.

Also before 1953 was a fortnight old, Representative Clair Engel (Democrat, California) had introduced a bill in the House that would authorize California to operate the Central Valley project under Federal reclamation law. He admitted that the state-ownership people would not be fully pleased, but he called state operation a step in the direction of state ownership, and hence a step toward the elimination of the offending acreage and power clauses. His bill paralleled in advance Attorney General Herbert Brownell's suggestion . . . that the states manage offshore oil production under continued Federal ownership.

We may expect more pressure for local ownership or local operation, more political support for the Corps of Engineers, whose projects are so opportunely uninhibited, more efforts to have acreage limitations voided on particular projects. The trick of playing off one bureau against another is as old as reclamation itself. Resisting it involves more than a simple defense of the Bureau of Reclamation against the Corps of Engineers, for conservation forces themselves are divided on the wisdom of some projects. Hydroelectric power sites do not last forever; they silt up or suffer impaired flow, and some must be conserved for the future. Moreover, the Hoover Commission's recommendation that Engineers and Reclamation Bureau be fused into one civilian agency meets not only bureau resistance but doubts among the friends of reclamation. The one point on which there is agreement among conservationists is that the Corps of Engineers should be brought under the same organic law, subject to the same restrictions and with the same obligation to enforce them, that the Bureau of Reclamation works under. Otherwise the whole program will be cracked open by political manipulations. . . .

The wider the base, said Alexander Hamilton, the better the democratic system will work. The more interests represented, the less danger there is that a single one will be able to dominate. Absentee landlordism of the Federal kind may sometimes suffer from insufficient information, but it is less subject to manipulation or subversion, and in questions of policy it almost invariably will take a broader view than local interests or local government.

PRIVATE FORESTRY IN TRANSITION [8]

From colonial days to the present, the forests of the United States have played a major role in its development. They have built its homes, supplied the raw material for many of its manufactured products, provided containers for their shipment, and helped to prevent erosion and floods. These products and services have come, and must continue to come, mainly from the three fourths of our forest area that is in private ownership. What are the prospects that this area of 345 million acres will be so managed as to guarantee adequate future supplies and services?

Until recently most students of the situation have viewed it with uneasy concern or even genuine alarm. For more

[8] From article by Samuel T. Dana, Filibert Roth University Professor of Forestry, University of Michigan. *Annals of the American Academy of Political and Social Science.* 281:84-92. May 1952. Reprinted by permission.

than half a century they have emphasized the key position in the national economy occupied by forest lands in private ownership, and have successively proposed public coopera- tion, public regulation, public ownership, and private initia- tive as means of assuring their effective management.[9]. . .

Status of Private Management

Where . . . does private forestry stand today, and what are its prospects for the future? Is the perennial problem of American forestry—management of private lands—actual- ly on its way to a satisfactory solution? Is the outlook as rosy as the optimists in industry believe, or as dark as the pessimists in government fear?

The answer to these questions, in the judgment of a middle-of-the-roader like the present writer, is that private forestry is in a state of transition from a position of minor importance in the national economy to one of major impor- tance. It has come a long way in recent years; it still has a long way to go; and liberal public participation in the for- estry enterprise will continue to be necessary for satis- factory progress.

Private forestry has gone farther in the last decade than in all the previous years of our history put together. The number of well-managed properties has jumped suddenly from the hundreds into the thousands. The rapidity of the change is dramatized by the growth in the number of tree farms from one in 1941 to more than thirty-five hundred today. . . .

According to AFPI [American Forest Products Insti- tute], the sponsor of the tree farm movement,

A tree farm is an area of privately owned forest land devoted primarily to the continuous growth of merchantable forest products under good forest practices. . . . Tree farming, like the raising of any crop, is a practical business venture.

[9] Professor Dana's discussion of (a) public cooperation and regulation pro- posed, (b) public ownership proposed, and (c) self-regulation, is omitted, due to limitations of space.—Ed.

Both the idea and the name have proved so popular that thirty-three states now have formal tree-farm programs. Each of these states has a responsible agency to establish and enforce standards of practice, compliance with which entitles an owner, whether of a small farm woodlot or a large industrial holding, to be officially certified as a tree farmer. . . .

Activities of the Industry

The new attitude is well stated on the letterhead of the country's largest private timberland owner: "Timber is a crop." It finds expression in the woods, both on tree farms and elsewhere, in more effective control of fire, insects, and disease; in thinnings, cleanings, and other silvicultural treatments in immature stands to improve quality of the final crop; in the conduct of harvesting operations so as to obtain natural reproduction of desirable species in adequate amount; in the artificial reforestation of denuded areas; in the development of permanent systems of transportation; and in the practice of sustained-yield management, through which the balancing of growth and drain assures continued forest production for an indefinite future. It also finds expression in the general acquisition by larger owners (especially in the paper industry) of small holdings which for economic reasons cannot be handled satisfactorily by their present owners and are likely to be much better managed as integral parts of an extensive timber-growing enterprise.

In some instances private management is even more intensive than that on national forests, where standards have long been high. Moreover, the Southern Pulpwood Conservation Association and several individual owners assist smaller owners without charge in the management of their land. Such assistance may include the marking of the trees to be cut in a logging operation and the furnishing of planting stock for reforestation purposes. This is not entirely an altruistic gesture, but rather an intelligent approach to the problem of assuring an adequate supply of wood to meet the manufacturer's needs for raw material.

All these activities are normally conducted under the professional direction of a trained forester, who may be on the staff of the owner, employed by him on a consulting basis, or made temporarily available in an advisory capacity by a public agency. Some 5,100 foresters are now estimated to be employed by industry. Several of the larger companies have a score or more of foresters on their payrolls, many in positions of responsibility for the determination of policy as well as of technical practice. A few concerns go so far as to employ specialists for research in such fields as forest pathology, forest entomology, and forest soils. Experimental forests, sometimes aggregating many thousand acres, are not uncommon. One of the most encouraging features of the situation is that current openings for foresters in private employ considerably exceed those in public employ.[10]. . .

Motivation of Advance

The important question is: How permanent and how effective is the recent upsurge in private forestry? In an economic world, it is encouraging that the primary cause of the new interest is an economic one. Owners have not suddenly "got religion" or become panicky because of fear of Federal regulation; nor are they unduly influenced by the opportunity to invest in their own business funds that would otherwise go to the government as income taxes. They have decided to go into the business of growing timber because it pays. High stumpage prices, the closer utilization of inferior material made possible by advances in wood technology, and the necessity of protecting heavy investments in land and mills now justify practices which most owners, rightly or wrongly, formerly regarded as uneconomical. Added to the economic motive, on the part of some at least of the larger manufacturers, is a sense of responsibility for the maintenance of the communities supported by their plants.

Enlightened self-interest thus provides a solid foundation which offers real promise of permanence. Another depres-

[10] A section devoted to the publicity work done by the AFPI and individual companies is omitted.—Ed.

sion would undoubtedly lead to some decrease in expenditures for forestry by private owners, just as it would lead to economies in other directions. That it would result in the virtual abandonment of any considerable part of the present program is most unlikely, particularly in the case of manufacturers with heavy capital investments. The stakes are too high.

Good But Not Good Enough

On the other hand, accomplishments to date in relation to needs give no cause for complacency. Forest Service estimates showing the status of forest management in 1945 are given . . . [below]. Additional areas have come under management since that date, and the intensity of management on other areas has no doubt increased.

CHARACTER OF CUTTING IN 1945
(Per cent)

	Good and Better	Fair	Poor and Worse
Private ownership	8	28	64
Small	4	25	71
Medium	8	31	61
Large	29	39	32
Public ownership	67	19	14
National forests	80	19	1
Other Federal	43	32	25
State and local	47	10	43
All lands	23	25	52

Even so, the level of management of the private forests is clearly low, both intrinsically and in comparison with that of the public forests. This is notably true of the small holdings (less than 5,000 acres) and the medium-sized holdings (5,000 to 50,000 acres), with only 4 and 8 per cent respectively under good or better management. The large owners, particularly the pulp and paper companies, are doing much better, with 29 per cent of the area involved under good or excellent management; but this group includes only 15 per cent of the total forest area in private ownership.

A closer look at the situation in one of the most productive forest areas in the country, the southern pine region, is revealing. Here the pulp and paper industry has increased its output nearly ten times in the last twenty years, with another marked expansion scheduled for the immediate future. Although pulp and paper manufacturers are almost uniformly practicing good forestry on their own lands, these are far from adequate to meet their requirements. They must therefore obtain about half of their wood supply, in competition with the lumber industry and other wood-using industries, from other lands. Of these, the most important are the small ownerships, which greatly predominate in the region, and only 2 per cent of which are being well handled. Clearly, the progress which has so far been made, spectacular as it is on some individual properties, is far from enough.

Forest Service estimates also show that the total growth of the forests (in cubic feet) approximately equals the total drain resulting from cutting and from losses by fire, insects, and disease, and that the growth of saw timber (in board feet) is about two thirds of the drain. Do these figures mean that more widespread and more intensive forest management, whether on public or private lands, is not really an urgent necessity? They mean no such thing, unless we are willing to reduce drastically our consumption of saw timber, on which we now depend for many important uses.

Wood, in spite of the much-advertised increase in the use of substitutes, continues to be the "universal raw material." Far from being "obsolete," it is constantly finding new uses and being improved for old uses. From lumber, plywood, and the myriad articles manufactured from them, to turpentine and rosin, paper and its products, lignin, sugar, alcohol, vanillin, and other chemical derivatives, forest products enter into our daily life not only in many obvious but also in many unrecognized ways. Our whole economy will be richer or poorer as they are abundant or scarce.

Liberal use of forest products is desirable because of their renewability as well as because of their utility. It is re-assuring to know that about a fourth of our total land area is best suited to the production of forest crops, and that these 461 million acres, if properly managed, would permanently provide a much larger yield than we are now harvesting.

The Social Requirement

Is any such addition to the national wealth in the form of increased forest production likely to result from private enterprise alone? In spite of the recent highly encouraging developments in private forestry, the answer is almost certainly No. The job is of a nature and a size to require public participation. There is nothing inconsistent with the "American way of life" in this conclusion.

The institutions of private property and private profit are based on the theory that they best serve the interests of society as a whole. Here in the United States we are con-vinced that this is the case; but when unrestricted freedom of enterprise fails to render optimum service or results in actual disservice, the community does not hesitate to inter-vene. Public schools, agricultural experiment stations, blue-sky laws, pure food and drug acts, regulation of public utility rates and service, incentive payments, zoning ordi-nances, control of stream pollution, and national parks, to pick just a few examples, all bear witness to this fact.

Experience both here and abroad shows that forestry is a field in which such intervention is often desirable. Many owners are either unable or unwilling to handle their lands in such a way as to assure their continued productivity. When forest supplies are abundant in relation to the demand, this fact may have little social significance. When the situa-tion becomes reversed, it may be of outstanding importance. Indeed, as population expands and natural resources shrink, the point may well be reached where the way in which they are managed is of more concern to the community at large than to their individual owners.

The United States cannot raise the standard of living for its own rapidly mounting population, nor can it exercise effective leadership in a bankrupt world, without wise use of its natural resources, among which forests are of major importance. The goal must be reached chiefly through action of private owners, but with a reasonable measure of the three forms of public participation with which we are already familiar.

Forms of Public Participation

Public cooperation is exemplified in such fields as protection of forests from fire, insects, and disease; research; education; provision of planting stock; and on-the-ground aid in the management of specific properties. These activities are almost universally approved, including the liberal use of Federal grants-in-aid administered by state agencies. They have demonstrated the ability of private owners and of Federal and state officials to work together in the formulation and execution of constructive programs in which the participation of all concerned is on a wholly voluntary basis.

Public regulation commands less favor, even at the state level; but it is likely to prove necessary, particularly in connection with "protection forests," unless forest owners as a whole prove more amenable to educational influences here than they have proved in even such forest-minded countries as Norway and Sweden. It is significant that in Oregon and Washington, which now have the most drastic laws of any of the states, the legislation had the backing of the very owners who were to be regulated; and that in Washington these owners helped to get a decision from the state Supreme Court upholding the constitutionality of the act. In the words of L. F. Watts, chief of the Forest Service, regulatory measures constitute the "rules of the game" and "are as necessary in resource management as they are to transportation, communication, and other enterprises that affect the public welfare." Although mandatory in form, the fact that they automatically force an owner to consider the basic problem of sustained forest production gives them great potential educational value, which is magnified if private owners themselves participate in the regulatory process.

Public ownership to the extent of 25 per cent of the commercial forest area has resulted from the reservation of lands originally in Federal or state ownership (chiefly the public domain), from the acquisition of additional lands by purchase or exchange, and by the retention of tax-delinquent lands. They include largely lands that are (or have been) submarginal for private ownership, and that are needed for purposes such as watershed protection and recreation,which are generally recognized as a public responsibility. The character of their management is less subject to the ups and downs of the business cycle than is the management of private lands, and they can be used for the production of timber of larger size and higher quality than most private owners can afford to grow. This latter function will continue to be an important one until the highly uncertain arrival of the day when technology makes it possible to substitute built-up and synthetic products for high-grade lumber and plywood with equal satisfaction from the standpoint of cost, utility, and beauty. That the present pattern of ownership is the best that could be devised is unlikely; but that a considerable backlog of public forests is highly desirable as a means of promoting stability and of providing intangible but essential services can hardly be doubted.

Summary

To sum up, private forestry is in a state of transition. Timber mining is at last being replaced by timber cropping on a substantial scale. Great credit is due to the individuals, companies, and organizations whose leadership has been responsible for the change. The evidence is convincing that the new attitude is here to stay, and that the movement which they have started will continue to spread.

Enthusiasm over recent progress should not, however, blind us to the fact that it is only a good beginning. Evolution, not revolution, is the order of the day. Neither the area of private forest land now under management nor the average quality of that management gives any assurance of a continuing supply of forest products adequate to meet the needs of a nation with a rapidly expanding population, a desire for ever higher standards of living, and a responsibility for world leadership. Current efforts by private owners must be intensified, extended, and supplemented (not supplanted) by appropriate activities on the part of public agencies.

Private forestry in the United States has come far in the last ten years. It has still farther to go. With full cooperation on the part of all concerned, there is reasonable hope of success in attaining the common objective of enabling our forest resources to play the part they can and should in promoting and maintaining the prosperity of the nation. Industry's present attitude arouses hope and confidence that the transition from negligible planned production, through substantial production, to full production on the 75 per cent of our forest area in private hands will be faster than we had dared to hope. The prospect is one to encourage optimism but not complacency.

V. ATOMIC ENERGY

EDITOR'S INTRODUCTION

When Congress passed the Atomic Energy Act in 1946, giving the Federal Government complete control of atomic energy development, the action was defended primarily on the basis of national security. Recently, however, in the controversy over the 1954 revision of the Act (Public Law 703, H.R.9757, Atomic Energy Act of 1954, approved August 30, 1954), the retention of government control has been urged for other reasons, perhaps the most important of which claims that the taxpayers, who have spent approximately $12 billion in developing atomic energy, should receive any benefits accruing therefrom.

Critics of the 1946 Act argued that national security was no longer best served by the government's attempts at secrecy and exclusion of private industry; that the government's monopoly, while in existence, impeded the development of atomic energy and thereby jeopardized our international position as well as retarded domestic, peacetime progress.

The first selection which follows describes the evolution of national atomic energy policy under the Atomic Energy Act, and the second analyzes the reasons for ending governmental control in favor of private industrial development. Retention of Federal control is urged in the next selection, largely because of the government's past investment in the field, but criticized, in the fourth article, on the basis that the government's monopoly prevents the rapid development which private business would provide. Next, Representative Price (speaking prior to the revision of the Act) questions the necessity and wisdom of a change in our national policy on atomic energy. "Industry Bids for Atomic Power," the last statement of opinion, summarizes the arguments for and against private ownership, concluding that "the time now seems appropriate and the climate of public thinking right to entrust future atomic power to the type of mind which has always contributed more to the public welfare than bureaucracy ever has or ever can."

THE ATOMIC ENERGY INDUSTRY: AN EXPERIMENT IN HYBRIDIZATION [1]

The Socialists contend rightly that certain forms of property should be reserved to the state, since possession of them carries with it a kind of power too great to be left to private individuals without grave danger to the community in general. Just demands of this sort contain nothing that is opposed to Christian truth.—Pope Pius XI, *Quadragesimo anno,* May 15, 1931.

Let me add that I think that the distinction is wisely drawn in S.1717 between the realm of discussion and experimentation, where freedom is the only safe rule, and the realm of applied technology, where, in a matter that involves the national safety and welfare so vitally, social control is essential. The control that S.1717 would impose upon the commercial production of fissionable materials and their utilization in industrial channels seems to me to be entirely justified. If the push of a button can destroy a city, no nation can afford to leave the button in private hands. That would amount to an abdication of sovereignty.—Secretary of the Interior Harold Ickes, testifying before Senate Special Committee on Atomic Energy.

The release of atomic energy confronted the nation with a unique problem in social control. Recognizing the dangers inherent in this vast new productive resource, Congress launched a major experiment in government: it established the Atomic Energy Commission to supervise atomic development as a Federal monopoly. The Commission . . . has engaged in research and production on a vast scale. Its plants, laboratories, depots, testing grounds and the like are not only spread over the nation but are located on distant islands in the Pacific. . . . Nevertheless, the American pub-

[1] From article by James R. Newman, member of the New York Bar. *Yale Law Journal.* 60:1263-1394. December 1951. Reprinted by permission.

lic, and even persons in responsible positions, have only the meagerest knowledge about the Commission's activities, even those phases which by no stretch of imagination may be considered as legitimately entitled to the prohibitions and protection of secrecy regulations. . . .

One may debate whether it was wise after the war to assign to the Federal Government the development as well as the control of atomic energy. A conservative Congress argued the question for months and answered it in the affirmative. To this conclusion they were driven, only reluctantly, by their concept of the requirements of national security. One may ask whether, regardless of military needs, this resource, brought to practical use with public monies, should not as a matter of course be further exploited for the common good as a public trust. President Truman, Senator McMahon [the late Brien McMahon, Democrat, Connecticut], and other leaders have taken this view; not a few have vigorously opposed it. One may suggest that the experience of the atomic energy program indicates the desirability of scrapping the main features of the Atomic Energy Act and opening the field for private development—subject only to regulatory scrutiny. Those who have urged such action— Mr. [David E.] Lilienthal [former chairman of the Atomic Energy Commission] is a notable exponent—assert that the security safeguards which the Seventy-ninth Congress had in the forefront of its thought in adopting the McMahon Act could be fully preserved at the same time the numerous advantages of private ownership and competition were conferred on the enterprise. Yet whatever may be debated, whatever questions are as yet unanswered, and issues unresolved, one fact is plain: a small but powerful segment of American industry is today the manager of the great bulk of the atomic energy program. Industry is operating the reactors and auxiliary plant at Hanford, the experimental power reactor at Knolls Point, the diffusion plants at Oak Ridge and Paducah, the tritium plant at Savannah, the materials testing reactors, the aircraft and submarine nuclear reactor programs; industry is producing plutonium, constructing factories and other installations, manufacturing and experimenting on weapons; industry is hiring, firing, fixing the wages and working conditions of 95 per cent of the atomic energy labor force; industry is running the communities; industry, in short, is making, expanding and learning the business of nuclear engineering. This is not a sinister fact; but it is a fact too little known, too little discussed, too little weighed. One may approve the present dispensation or deplore it; one can scarcely afford to neglect its implications.

The McMahon Act has from time to time been denounced as socialistic. It may be admitted that initially, and theoretically, this was its tendency—though mention of the word itself caused to shudder those who most ardently supported the bill in Congress. Nonetheless the majority took the position that even if the bill was the quintessence of Bolshevism, if it was essential to military security, it should be passed. (General Eisenhower, it is worth remarking, strongly urged its adoption—a factor of major importance in determining the final vote). But as the Act has been carried out, it is doubtful that Prince Metternich would have had reason to be alarmed over its revolutionary character. In all spheres of its responsibility the Commission consistently has striven to relieve itself of the odious encumbrance of monopoly, to reduce its scope, to delegate authority, to divest itself of control, to prepare the way for the entry of private industry. The AEC has shown its contractors unremitting solicitude, being thoughtful alike of their present interest and their future aspirations. They have had no cause for dissatisfaction and indeed they have voiced none. From conversations with certain industry officials I gather they have been somewhat amused, if not puzzled, at the laments of publicists over the alleged exclusion of private industry from participation in the atomic energy project. It must be conceded, to be sure, that some large firms which desired to take part in the work have been left in the cold. But it was not the *Federal* monopoly that froze them out. While this fact may not offer much consolation, it puts matters in a different light. The Federal monopoly already having been transformed into a hybrid partnership in which private companies run most of the business while the AEC furnishes the money, there is sound basis for the expectation that not too long hence government will leave the partnership entirely, becoming, instead, the ideal customer—prepared both to subsidize and to buy the entire product of the business. In that event, there would be room for other private partners. There is ample evidence that this course is in contemplation. Studies are now underway as to how the plutonium business might be put on a profit basis. The Commission is aware of shortcomings in its manufacturing record: waste, extravagance, serious lags in certain spheres of technology, and other forms of inefficiency. These blemishes, it is felt, would vanish under "the play of industrial initiative." The impelling motive for the change is, of course, the "national defense." But it is suggested also that if industry were to take over, the "broad commercial use" of atomic energy would be accelerated.

Observe the curious evolution of national atomic energy policy. The initial predilection was to abrogate the wartime system, to eliminate the state from all but regulatory control, and to open the new resource to private industrial exploitation. Such a policy was opposed mainly on the grounds that it would jeopardize the nation's military defenses. Thereafter control legislation was adopted removing atomic energy from the domain of private enterprise. The control agency adhered to the formal requirements of the statute but provided for private participation by means of management contracts and other devices. After a few years of experience along this line, it is now suggested that the Federal monopoly is itself the principal cause of shortcoming in the production program and that, so far from private exploitation of atomic energy weakening the country militarily, the transfer of the program to competitive enterprise would fortify security. In short the Atomic Energy Act adopted in the interest of national defense is now to be repealed in the interest of national defense. Symmetrical and very neat—but not very convincing. It is prudent to doubt that the gravest defects in the program are the outgrowth of Federal monopoly; it is even less reasonable to anticipate their disappearance when private business takes over. The problems of labor relations, to cite only one example, are not so easily solved. Moreover, the major social, economic, and international considerations relating to the development of atomic energy, expressly recognized in the Act itself, appear to have been forgotten in the plangent urge to instate the enterprise system. And what has happened, one may ask, to the innocent notion that the benefits of atomic energy should accrue to the nation as a whole —without the prior drain of private profits—since the resource itself was brought to fruition by public funds? Somewhere along the circular route of national policy this point got lost. Sooner or later the American people will demand to know where and why. The answer, I venture to say, will not be easy to frame.

SHOULD WE BREAK OUR BIGGEST MONOPOLY? [2]

The biggest industrial monopoly in America—some $10 billion have been invested in it—is the monopoly in the ownership and processing of fissionable materials. . . .

The most important reason for establishing the monopoly initially was undoubtedly *security*. We did not want actual or potential national enemies, or even private citizens, to get hold of atomic weapons. There was also the feeling that the development of atomic energy was too big, or in some ways too revolutionary a thing for private enterprise. This feeling reflects what may be called the "Socialist" prejudice, and is usually based on a failure to understand how the general welfare might best be served by competitive private enterprise.

The opposite prejudice, which may be called the "laissez faire" prejudice, causes people to see good only in private

[2] Article by Abba P. Lerner, economist and professor of economics at Roosevelt College, Chicago. *Bulletin of the Atomic Scientists.* 9:110-14+. May 1953. Reprinted by permission.

enterprise, and to condemn public enterprise out of hand wherever it is not dictated by special considerations, like national security.

At the risk of appearing obvious, I shall try to enumerate and analyze the main objectives of nuclear development; and, at the risk of antagonizing the addicts of both prejudices, I shall try to show what policies would seem to be indicated if neither prejudice were permitted undue influence.

Objectives

The main objectives of any program for the development of atomic power are:

Development—We must hasten the technical development of nuclear energy, so that we may supply power (essentially, electrical) for industrial and domestic use and make such power cheap and widely available.

Safety—We must provide protection against the hazards of radiation and possible explosions for the workers in nuclear energy and the surrounding communities.

Security—1. Domestic. We must prevent any private individuals or groups from obtaining atomic weapons which then could be used for private or political terrorism.

2. International. We must strengthen as far as possible our ability to deter, or failing that, to defeat, aggression against our country or our allies, and to achieve victory with the minimum of danger to the civilization of free people. This can be accomplished by *military security* (acquiring many nuclear weapons for ourselves and preventing the possible enemy from learning our military secrets) and by *political security* (developing our economic strength; winning and keeping allies by helping them to prosperity, security, and freedom; carrying on a moral offensive directed toward detaching allies from the enemy so as to break down his political system and ultimately, perhaps, change him from an enemy into a friend).

Private Development Versus Security

. . . As long as fossil fuels remain a cheap source of power, nuclear power does not offer us much. Its importance lies in permitting a postponement of the transition from fuel energy to solar energy. Current estimates place the completion of the transition somewhere between one and three centuries from now in the absence of any nuclear power. Utilizing nuclear power, the transition may be postponed for more than one century, but probably for less than ten. . . .

The importance of nuclear power should not be underestimated just because one does not get easily excited about the postponement of a difficulty which in any case will not occur for a couple of centuries. The exhaustion of fossil fuels is a gradual process, and it has already reached a serious stage. In a few years, there will be places where using nuclear power will reduce costs; it will take a couple of centuries before this situation becomes universal.

The advantage of keeping our power cheap—perhaps, for as long as a thousand years—is nevertheless, less important than providing safety and security for a free society, in which alone the ideals of our civilization can be preserved and developed. How much less important, then, is the actual issue of *development,* which is not whether nuclear power should be utilized at all during the next thousand years, but merely whether its use should be pushed forward during the next ten or twenty years? Certainly, if there is a serious conflict between the objectives, considerations of *safety* and *security* should prevail over those of a possible speeding up of atomic power development by private enterprise.

Another argument against "handing over atomic power to private enterprise," is that the taxpayer, having invested some $10 billion in atomic energy, has a vested right in any profits that might result from this investment, and private enterprise should not be permitted to appropriate these profits. It is further argued that public utilities might want to control atomic power so as to prevent competition with power supplied from conventional sources; and a special danger is seen in the proposal that private firms should produce plutonium and power, and sell their plutonium to the Atomic Energy Commission. Whether this power is cheap would then depend upon the price received for the plutonium. Not only is there a likelihood of a hidden subsidy in this situation, but also the danger of a vested interest being developed in continued purchases of plutonium by the military establishment. The firms using cheap energy (made by the income from the sale of plutonium), workers in the firms using this cheap power, businessmen providing these workers with housing, groceries, and amusement—all these would apply political pressure to force the government to continue to purchase the plutonium that keeps down the price of power. This would result not only in a wasteful subsidy, but also in an incarnation of the fable of the "merchants of death"—the story of weapons which accumulated because of economic interests, until war began almost automatically!

Private Development Aids Security

Under close examination, however, . . . these arguments against private enterprise in atomic power lose much of their effectiveness. In the first place, there is no clear conflict between *security* and *development*. Even if we approach *security* in the narrow military sense, the enlistment of private enterprise in *development* may yield us more or better weapons simply because Atomic Energy Commission men would be free to concentrate on weapon research. There is even less of a conflict if we approach *security* in the broader political sense. The winning and keeping of allies in the world struggle is to a large extent the problem of helping them avoid the disorganization and despair that may turn them to our enemies for assistance. In this situation, rapid development of nuclear energy could in many cases contribute spectacularly. Many parts of the world which are politically uncertain are areas where power is expensive and where nuclear power might prove important.

Probably even more significant than the economic benefits that such areas could enjoy from the nuclear power plants we may be able to supply, would be the demonstration of our peaceful use of the atom. Such a demonstration would help swing the neutral countries to our side, and could even contribute to the disintegration of the enemy's satellite system. In this way, we could transform enemies into friends.

The argument that emphasizes the taxpayer's vested interest in the $10 billion invested in atomic energy overlooks the fact that most of this money was devoted to the rapid production of nuclear weapons. Furthermore, it seems to be based on a belief that the general public would benefit more from the development of nuclear power if private firms are *not* permitted to enter the field. In nuclear development—as in any other field—the public can only benefit from private investment. The investment, by increasing the demand for goods and services, raises the prices that the public receives for them; and by increasing the supply of power, it reduces the price that the public has to pay.

There is more substance to the argument that public utilities might want to control atomic energy in order to suppress a competitor, that when public enterprise retires from nuclear energy, private enterprise will be permitted to sabotage it. It should be noted that this is not an objection against private enterprise *utilizing* nuclear fission, but rather against *inadequate* utilization. Keeping private enterprise out of atomic power altogether will not permit it to make *any* use of the new process. The problem is not how to prevent private investment in nuclear power, but how to insure that the new processes are indeed utilized for the public benefit. This could be done by insuring sufficient private competition to make suppression impossible, by having public competition on fair terms, or by such regulations of the industry as will provide a satisfactory service. . . .

Rational Calculation

The establishment of nuclear power plants abroad . . . raises serious questions of *security* in the narrow or military sense. There would be some danger of military secrets being learned by the enemy and of the fissionable material being captured and perhaps made into nuclear weapons to be used against us. However, security in the broader sense may benefit if we gave a nuclear power plant to an energy-hungry country; and this advantage may far outweigh the loss of security in the narrow sense from the possibility of some uranium being captured by the enemy. This would seem more and more likely as we and the enemy approach the "optimum" stockpile of nuclear weapons. In all such cases the dangers must be estimated and weighed against the benefits.

This brings us to the more positive and more distinctive way in which the utilization of private enterprise for *development* can help *security* in the broad sense. I refer to the connection between private enterprise and the rational procedure of weighing and calculating advantages and disadvantages—of vigilant observation to see whether there is too much of this or too little of that, to bring about the greatest profit or other benefit.

One of the most serious weaknesses of governmental action is the habit of exalting some very important consideration, such as the consideration of security, into a "super-priority." It would be a great contribution toward the achievement of all our objectives, if the contact with private enterprise would lead to the transformation of *security* from an absolute criterion to a commodity subject to rational quantification—to the modes of more and less.

Secrecy Versus Security

One element in security is secrecy, but too often security is *identified* with secrecy. When we had the monopoly of nuclear weapons, it was difficult to imagine any degree of secrecy being too great. But since there does no longer seem to be any basic secret, it does seem to an outsider that we may very well be enjoying too much secrecy for our own good.

With the degree of secrecy that is at present being applied to nuclear power production, the entry of private enterprise into the field can take the form of only a few large firms with their stable personnel, having some of its men cleared for handling classified information and fissionable materials, so that they may be able to make bids for possible contracts. If private enterprise can work only in this limited and clumsy way, there is little difference between this kind of operation and having the men employed directly by the AEC.

The great argument for private enterprise is that it permits adventurous men to try out methods which would be rejected in a nationalized (or in any other) bureaucratic setup. The kind of private enterprise just described hardly supports this argument.

This is not to say that a few private firms would not do some good. To have even two competing enterprises is better than having a complete monopoly. But this kind of competition might just as well be set up between different parts of the AEC, except that the introduction of competing private firms will increase the available amount of scientific and engineering talent and management skills.

If it should be decided, as a result of the infection of the AEC with the calculating habits of competitive private enterprise, that secrecy has indeed been carried too far and is unduly hindering *development*, it might be possible to utilize private enterprise in a more effective manner. For example, it might be made a practice for nuclear engineers to have their loyalty and reliability checked when (or before) they get their training. If enough such men were cleared for classified information, and if they were sufficiently protected from the temptation of becoming spies, they might be able to experiment with unorthodox procedures as members of independent firms, bidding for small parts of any aggregate undertaking without having first to convince ranks upon ranks of inevitably timid bureaucrats. They would be able to win great rewards if they turn out right and go bankrupt if they turn out wrong.

It is impossible, of course, for an outsider to say whether this would indeed be practical, but only to the degree that something of this kind can be made to happen, is there much substance to the cry that bringing in private enterprise is likely to lead to more rapid development of atomic power.

Too Much Safety

It has been suggested that the AEC has permitted *safety* to exceed the rational limit. It does, of course, seem heartless to say that the AEC workers should have been less thoroughly protected from hazards, but the lives of other workers also are precious, and they, too, have wives and children and should also be protected from accidents. There are limits to the resources that can be applied to this purpose—as to any other purpose. What is unquestionably desirable is that the resources that are available for such a purpose should be used as effectively as possible, so as to minimize the total number of accidents everywhere.

Because of this, it is possible that the AEC has been providing too much *safety*. I do not know, of course, whether that is the case, but the test is relatively easy. If a million dollars could be expended elsewhere to safeguard people from accidents, say, in protecting level crossings, or in providing machinery guards, and if used in this way this sum could prevent more accidents than would be caused by taking a million dollars away from safety expenditure in the AEC, then it would be desirable to spend the million dollars in those other places rather than in the AEC. Given the total available expenditure for accident prevention, the statement that there is too much *safety* in the AEC is equivalent to the less shocking statement that there is too little safety in the other places. An important benefit from the utilization of private enterprise in *development* would be the necessity for having safety regulations which would be more uniform throughout the industry. This would give more over-all protection for any given quantity of resources made available for the purpose. It might also show that the costs of atomic power have been unduly inflated by this error.

Finally, the spirit of rational quantitative calculation might also be applied to the question of how much private and how much public enterprise is desirable. This would of course mean the overcoming of the two basic prejudices mentioned at the beginning of this article, and taking the position that neither private nor public enterprise should be favored, but that they should have to compete with each other on equal basis. Private yardsticks should be utilized in judging public enterprise—just as public yardsticks may be utilized in judging private enterprise.

This means that subject to proper inspection and control against the misappropriation of fissionable material (for gangsters, or for foreign governments) and for the safeguarding of military secrets, private enterprise should be permitted to participate not only in the production of electric power from atomic energy, but also in the running of nuclear reactors that produce the heat for transformation into power, and indeed, in the manufacture of atomic weapons: in short, in every activity in which their competition would be effective. On the other hand, by the same token, no activities should be barred to public enterprise—provided it is made to compete against private enterprise in a completely fair contest: i.e., both being subject to the same regulations, taxes, subsidies, etc.

Ownership of Fissionable Materials

The Atomic Energy Act of 1946 prohibits the private *ownership* of fissionable materials (Section 5, *a*, 2) or of any facilities that could produce fissionable materials in dangerous quantities (Section 4, *a*, 1). These provisions were presumably directed towards *safety* and *security*. It is of interest that in the foregoing discussion in this article, there was no occasion to consider the question of private or public ownership either of fissionable materials or of the facilities for producing it.

This is because ownership is not important. What is important is *security*, both domestic and international, so that it is access to nuclear weapons and fissionable materials and the possibility of these being misappropriated, that are the dangers that matter—not ownership.

This irrelevant concern about ownership is also found in discussions about arranging for private firms to participate in atomic power development. Much has been made of the necessity of changing the law so that firms may be permitted to own nuclear reactors if they are to find out how to run them and redesign them for greater efficiency and economy. But no firm could object to the AEC or the FBI guarding a privately owned reactor, keeping a continuous watch to see that none of the plutonium is secretly removed, or making sure that the safety regulations were being observed. On the other hand, if a private firm contracted to work on a reactor belonging to the AEC there would be no reason why the AEC should want to interfere with anything the firm wanted to do which did not affect *safety* and *security*, but which might lead to improved efficiency and economy from which the firm would gain under its contract and from which everybody would gain in the long run. I therefore find it difficult, in fact impossible, to see what difference it would make to anyone whether the reactor was said to belong to the AEC, or to the private firm.

If I am right, this brings out most dramatically the impropriety of both the "Socialist" and the "laissez faire" prejudices. We have already seen that they both interfere with the choice between private and public enterprise on the only point which is relevant—that of efficiency. Thus, it turns out that once we define what may and may not be allowed, we see that the question of private or public ownership fades into insignificance if not actual meaninglessness. . . .

Conclusions

Our objectives for nuclear plans are *development, safety,* and *security.* Although the rapid development of atomic power through private enterprise is the least important of them and should be sacrificed as an objective if there is serious conflict, it seems that development is more likely to help than to hinder the other objectives.

If we can overcome the prejudices that cause some to view with alarm the "handing over of atomic energy to private interests" and cause others to condemn public enterprise in any field where private enterprise could possibly be used, we must conclude that neither form of enterprise should be favored above the other, so that in every instance, the competition will be won by the enterprises, private or public, that are most efficient.

Security must be protected in the same way whether the enterprise is public or private and whether the fissionable materials, etc., are considered to be private or public property.

Once the necessary *safety* and *security* regulations are set up for general application, *everything* should be tried— large as well as small reactors; public, private, as well as mixed enterprises; reactors producing only power, or only plutonium, or both together; reactors and power plants, large and small, to be sent to approved energy-hungry countries; and anything else that seems attractive either to the AEC or to private firms.

This may have been undesirable up to now, while the need for a rapid assembling of a minimum stockpile of nuclear weapons superseded all other considerations. Now that it seems to have been established that the supply of nuclear fuels is large and that the tightness in the supply of labor and critical industrial materials is disappearing, we may be able to explore many of these possibilities without endangering *security.* The most promising development is the one that would loosen unnecessary secrecy and offer a wider dissemination of materials that now remain classified to security-cleared nuclear engineers, so that there might perhaps be a movement toward real competition and real individual enterprise by daring minds who would like to back their own unorthodox ideas.

WHOSE ATOM IS IT? [3]

The greatest giveaway of all, of course, is the atomic-energy giveaway. Involved are sums which are incalculable. . . . The nation's water-power resources are sixteen times greater than all our coal, oil, and natural-gas reserves put together. But potentially the energy of the waterfall is as nothing compared to that of the atom, in which is imprisoned the energy that may one day prove the source of all power on earth. This is the nature of the energy source which the Atomic Energy Act of 1954 takes away from the public domain and in large measure hands over to private interests.

It is impossible to place a dollar value on this deal. Yet in an account which is a kind of audit one must choose some figure to start with. The most appropriate is perhaps the $12 billion of public money which the government has spent so far on its atomic-energy program, the fruits of which, under the new bill, now go to the private power interests.

"Make no mistake about it," warned Senator Morse [former Independent, now Democrat, Oregon], during the debate on the bill, ". . . [this] is definitely and primarily a power bill, but it is a bill designed to turn over the power features of the atomic-energy program to private industry rather than to guard the public interest in its $12 billion investment in atomic-energy production." This is the most important fact about the Atomic Energy Act of 1954: it is a bill dealing with power—mainly electric power.

A statement prepared by the Federal Power Commission for the Joint Committee on Atomic Energy . . . made this very clear:

Current proposals to develop peacetime uses of atomic energy may involve some of the same problems faced in 1908, when Federal

[3] From editorial in *Nation.* 179:278-9. October 2, 1954. Reprinted by permission.

water-power legislation was first proposed, and resolved in 1920, when the Federal Water Power Act was enacted. For by 1908 the nation had in water power, as it now has in atomic energy, a great energy resource, largely undeveloped but believed to be potentially very valuable.

The same fact was stated more forcefully by Senator Gore [Democrat, Tennessee] on July 22 . . . [1954]:

Practically everyone will admit that falling water and navigable streams are natural resources which belong to all the people. There are those, however, who argue that atomic energy does not fall within this category. I submit that it does, because the people have paid $12 billion for the development of this new resource; it is just as much a property of the people of the nation as is the falling water in a stream. The people through their government have discovered and developed this new source of energy; no private corporation can rightfully lay claim to it. The McMahon Act confirmed that principle when it vested in the government title to fissionable materials and nuclear processes.

As first reported back to the Senate from committee, the new bill, entitled Revisions to the Atomic Energy Act of 1946, made possible the crudest kind of giveaway to big business and the private utilities. There was no preference clause, a provision found in every public power law for the past fifty years insuring to co-ops, municipalities, and other public groups priority to power generated at government sources. The Atomic Energy Commission was not empowered to supply its own atomic-power plants with electric energy; private companies would furnish it. Private companies licensed to use atomic energy to create electric power were not placed under the regulatory provisions of the Federal Power Act. Private companies were permitted to take out patent rights on atomic energy after an almost meaningless buffer period of five years, during which all patents would be openly shared by all comers.

The original bill as reported in joint committee was, to quote Representatives Chet Holifield [Democrat, California] and Melvin Price [Democrat, Illinois] in their dissenting report, "barren of any recognition of the public interest in securing electric energy from this new resource at the lowest

possible rates." "Experience has shown," the two congressmen added, "that such regulatory authority is entirely inadequate to protect the public interest in electric power developed from public resources unless supplemented by specific
standards governing licenses and the availability of public or
cooperative competition in the distribution of electric
energy."

Because of the fight by Representatives Holifield and
Price, and Senators Gore, Morse, Magnuson [Democrat,
Washington], Monroney [Democrat, Oklahoma], Lehman
[Democrat, New York], and a few others, many of the
bill's original inadequacies were finally modified in the public's favor; the buffer period, however, was simply lengthened
from five to ten years. It is still an almost meaningless
provision. It is also the fulcrum for the great atomic giveaway.

One thing that makes the atomic-energy law a giveaway
is the very cost of atomic energy. The Federal Government
has had to spend $12 billion so far—more than private in-
dustry could have ever hoped to spend—on basic research and
military production. Only a few of the industrial giants
were able to participate jointly with the government in research—with the government footing the bill.

Under the new law, the Atomic Energy Commission will
issue licenses to private firms for development of commercial
uses of the atom. It is assumed by the bill's authors that
since a license may be issued to any person or firm which
meets the qualifications, everyone has an equal opportunity
to get a license. "Such an assumption ignores the development of the atomic program from the effectuation of the
1946 act until now," says Senator Gore. "It is painfully
plain that those few corporations which have been privileged
to be on the inside on research which has taken place to date
will have a head start on those not so fortunately situated."

This statement was supported by Senator Magnuson of
Washington during Senate debate of the bill. Its truth, he
said, had recently been apparent at the Hanover atomic-
energy plant, where "only two corporations" were "consid-

ered in the negotiations, General Electric and Westinghouse . . . those two corporations, that is all, in all of the negotiations with the commission."

Under the McMahon Act of 1946 all patents on inventions and discoveries useful in the production of fissionable material were outlawed. Patents were allowed in the so-called non-military field but were subject to a "public-interest declaration" which represented a form of compulsory licensing. In effect all firms were automatically granted permission to use the invention or discovery. Under the new act the same compulsory licensing is required, but only for ten years. After that all patents go out of the public domain. Since no one expects private atomic-energy plants to be in operation before another five or ten years, the provision is obviously suspect.

Originally, when the bill provided for only a five-year compulsory licensing period, Senator Gore said:

The five-year compulsory licensing aspect of the bill is an open invitation to evasion of the intent of Congress. It is completely unenforceable. . . .

All of the development accomplished so far is a product of government financing. Most of the development which will occur in the next five years will likewise be a product of government financing. It can be argued that a discovery conceived during a period in which the discoverer is subsidized by the government will still, even under the pending bill, be property of the government. But it must be remembered that patents are based upon discoveries and discoveries result from ideas. Who is to say at what specific time an idea was conceived?

Whatever loopholes existed in the five-year proviso, therefore, still exist in the ten-year proviso. Obviously, the reasonable thing for Congress to do would have been to retain the McMahon Act's compulsory licensing and wait a few years to determine when it should end. Instead, the existing clause was steam-rollered through by the Republicans.

A hint of things to come can be found in testimony given . . . before the Joint Committee on Atomic Energy by Alfred Iddles, president of the Babcock and Wilcox Company, one of the companies now participating in the atomic-energy program. Iddles admitted to Representative Holifield: "I know of several instances in which companies have had bright ideas that they have not divulged to anybody because they would not give them out." Later in the hearing the following exchange took place:

Holifield: So during this period of time when we are developing these reactors, which you say will possibly be from five to ten years, there will be no protection to the government against favored participants patenting these processes or mechanical inventions, even though the five-year compulsory licensing is put into the act.

Iddles: Would you have it otherwise?

Interestingly enough, only nine days after this Iddles wrote a letter to the joint committee asking that his answers to Representative Holifield be erased from his testimony. But it was too late. As Wayne Morse said later, he had "let the cat out of the bag."

HOW TO GET ATOMIC POWER FASTEST [4]

There should be no disparagement of President Eisenhower's proposal for an international atomic agency. Such an agency is immensely desirable as a method for promoting the spirit of peaceful international cooperation. Nevertheless, the President's proposal, if misinterpreted, could be dangerous. It could lull us Americans into doing less than we ought toward atomic-power development through our own national efforts.

What ought we to be doing? Two things:

One. We should spend much more money than we are now spending and make much more speed than we are now making in atomic-power experiments by our own government's Atomic Energy Commission.

Two. To come to top speed, we should call in American private firms to make atomic-power experiments with their own private funds.

[4] From article by William Hard, roving editor, *Reader's Digest.* *Reader's Digest.* 64:68-72. March 1954. Reprinted by permission.

We are today far from successful [in developing] atomic power for peaceful uses. What is our American record at this writing? We have derived tiny driblets of power from AEC nuclear reactors—"atomic furnaces"—in Idaho and in Tennessee. We have completed a reactor for installation in the recently launched *war* submarine, *Nautilus,* and we are preparing a second for a larger submarine. Studies are going forward for the development of reactors to provide propulsion for *war* aircraft and *war* aircraft carriers. But we do not today possess even one reactor for the production of land-based electric light and power for large-scale *civilian peaceful* use. And here's a startling fact:

When the President's Budget came to Congress last spring [1953] it contained not one penny for the construction of any such reactor. Whereupon the Congressional Joint Committee on Atomic Energy, headed by Representative Sterling Cole [Republican] of New York, took action and persuaded Congress to authorize a start on a reactor—called the PWR—for land-based civilian power purposes. This is progress; but the PWR will not be in operation for three or four more years. . . .

I cannot believe that the Communists who govern Russia will ever subordinate their pursuit of Communist atomic power to an international cooperative endeavor in which they would be helping to strengthen capitalistic atomic power. I think that we have to oppose our inventive might to theirs. Theirs is one single governmental aggregated might. We have something—if we will use it—that is stronger: the diffused and competitive inventive might of American private industry.

I thereupon thank our American stars for the policies pursued toward private industry by the Atomic Energy Commission. That commission is one of the best-manned and least bureaucratic agencies that Washington has ever seen. It has fewer than seven thousand employees. It operates most of its vast establishments through private firms called "operating contractors." There are more than a score of these, some small, some very big. Their employees number more than seventy thousand. Another score of private firms are serving the commission as "research and development contractors."

Some fifty firms have been authorized by the commission to pursue "studies" in the development of designs for reactors to produce power. Some twenty-seven of these are in a group headed by the Dow Chemical Company and the Detroit Edison Company of Michigan. This group, by the end of . . . [1954], will have backed its "study" by spending $4 million of its own money. . . .

Most of the veteran advocates of public electric power, Federal or state or municipal, are determined to keep atomic power a public monopoly. If they can do so, then, in time, when the atomic age comes into full flower, the Federal Government will come close to being the one great producer and purveyor of power in the whole United States. The prize is colossal; and the battle for it will be terrific.

So let us try to look at the problem without too much bigotry either way.

In the first place, nobody is suggesting that the AEC cease spending money on power reactors of its own. On the contrary, it is generally felt that the sums so far spent are pitifully small. The commission's one full-scale civilian power reactor—the PWR—will cost tens of millions of dollars. The magazine of the atomic industry, *Nucleonics*, reports:

> A key reactor authority thinks it will cost several hundred millions of dollars, including research and pilot-plant work, to get to the point where construction could be started on what could be predicted to be an *economic* power reactor.

Private industry cannot raise such sums till there is further proof that an atomic-power plant has a chance of being truly economic—that is, of being ultimately *competitive* with plants fueled by coal, gas or oil. Therefore, the Atomic Energy Commission still has a heavy task ahead of it in trying to make the atom constructive as well as destructive.

It would be a misfortune if any idea of "economy" prevented Congress from appropriating the sums necessary for us to achieve the world's most sought-after goal: successful civilian atomic power.

But what then should be the simultaneous role of American private industry? I see it in several phases.

One. Private industry should seriously consider a suggestion recently made by Representative Cole. He urged industry to invest private funds in constructing small-scale special-purpose reactors for disaster-struck areas, for bombed-out ports, for advanced military bases, such as the one at Thule, Greenland.

Opponents of private industry in the atomic-power field are always telling Congress: Private industry is not yet ready to begin. It is not yet ready to say what it will do. . . .

Should not private industry answer . . . boldly and adventurously? For at Thule, today, fuel oil for power has to be hauled in tankers thousands of miles. The cost of power is enormous: four cents a kilowatt-hour. Leading experts believe that a "package" atomic reactor, costing only a few million dollars, *might* beat that price—and make money. . . .

Two. Private industry should make it clear that it wants no monopoly of atomic power in the hands of a few companies. The group headed by Dow Chemical and Detroit Edison has stated that, "if the technical problems can be resolved," it wishes, "as soon as possible," to build and operate a reactor for private power without any public subsidies whatsoever. There should be many such groups with similar declared intentions. With these groups competing against one another there could be no monopoly of reactor design or practice.

Three. Private industry should make it plain that its rates for the sale of atomic power will be fixed by state and local public regulatory bodies. And, further, it should take the lead in explaining to the country that its use of atomic fuels will be strictly regulated by the Atomic Energy Commission.

Atomic fuels, like the so-called "ether" which carries radio waves, should always lie in the public domain. I can remember when private broadcasting companies seemed to think they could broadcast through the "ether" at random. Herbert Hoover, as Secretary of Commerce, quenched that idea, saw to it that each broadcasting company was confined to its own channel. Today all broadcasters are regulated in their use of the "ether" by the Federal Communications Commission. There is bound to be a similar regulation of the use of atomic fuels by the Atomic Energy Commission. Private atomic-power outfits will always be under thorough public control.

So I do not fear them. I welcome them. And I applaud a remark made some years back by Lewis L. Strauss, chairman of the AEC, a man who has the moral confidence of both political parties in Congress. He said:

"It is my hope that atomic energy can be freed of government monopoly and placed in the framework of the American system of free competitive enterprise."

And to the friends of government monopoly of atomic power I respectfully recall a historic incident recently mentioned by David E. Lilienthal, first chairman of the AEC. The United States Navy, at the end of World War I, concluded that all "wireless"—all "radio"—was essential to military security and should always remain in government ownership. And Mr. Lilienthal asks: Where now would be our radio industry, our television industry, our whole electronics industry, if their development had been left exclusively to a government bureau?

The other day the FCC adopted a set of standards for the successful promotion of color television. Where did it get them? From the pooled technical experiments and exertions of more than forty private competitive electronics companies.

I dare to predict similarly spectacular results for the public benefit from a privately owned and publicly regulated atomic-power industry. And the atom of peace is not only for power. It is for an almost infinite variety of uses— biological, medical, mechanical—the precise scope and reach of which no one set of minds, Russian or American, can possibly foresee. Fortunately, we Americans can open the task to multitudinous groups of minds competing freely against one another in separate imaginations toward the yet unimaginable end.

That is the course of freedom; and that is the course that will bring the blessings of the atom fastest to the world.

ARE WE READY TO GIVE THE ATOM TO PRIVATE ENTERPRISE? [5]

Mr. Speaker, has the time arrived for private enterprise to enter atomic power development on an independent basis? Featured articles in national magazines . . . create in the minds of the reader an affirmative answer. In my judgment, these articles are too optimistic and I believe that they have confused the public mind. Whether this confusion was deliberately or innocently caused may be subject to debate, but I believe the important point is to clear up the confusion. As a member—for over six years—on the Joint Committee on Atomic Energy, I deem it my duty to speak on this important matter.

Private Enterprise Has Been Given the Principal Job

Let me begin by stating that I am heartily in favor of private enterprise participation in all phases of the atomic research and development program. I have vigorously supported the principle which has been followed by the Atomic Energy Commission, for example, contractual arrangements with college and private laboratories for research and development, contractual arrangements with industrial and business management concerns in the fields of plant construction and plant operation. This principle has been applied as a basic policy by the Atomic Energy Commission.

[5] From address by Representative Melvin Price (Democrat, Illinois), delivered in the House of Representatives on June 10, 1953. Text from *Vital Speeches of the Day.* 19:562-6. July 1, 1953. Reprinted by permission.

Representatives of private industry have again and again testified before the Joint Committee on Atomic Energy and expressed their complete satisfaction with the cooperative attitudes and actions of the Atomic Energy Commission on this point. Private contractors have been given full rein to exercise their skill, ingenuity, managerial ability, and initiative. The Congress through appropriations has furnished over $12 billion for plant facilities and operational expenses. While it is true that an attempt has been made to eliminate private profits particularly on the operational level—no one can say that the private profit motive has been eliminated—construction of plants and interior equipment running into several billion dollars have contained profits for private construction companies and manufacturers of machinery.

In the operation of atomic plants customary business profits have not always been allowed, but in this field, great companies such as General Electric, Westinghouse, Union Carbon & Carbide, and hundreds of other industrial companies have obtained tangible benefits in chemical, metallurgical, and mechanical fields. They have gained organizational and managerial experience in basic scientific research and development, where discoveries of gadgets and processes have been made which were of direct value to their own commercial enterprises. The release of over five hundred patents by the Atomic Energy Commission is proof of my statement. There is also an important advantage in being first in any new industry and these companies know it.

A Cooperative Effort

I do not wish to detract from or minimize the great contribution which private enterprise has made in the atomic field. They are entitled to the praise and gratitude of every taxpayer in the United States, and the people of the free world. I seek only to set forth the facts and the facts would not be complete if I did not state further—if free enterprise has contributed, as they have, greatly to atomic development—it has been possible only because of the $12 billion in taxes which have been contributed by the United States taxpayer.

It has been a cooperative contribution for the preservation of liberty and if there be dollar benefits in the future, let them accrue fairly and justly to all the cooperative contributors, the taxpayers who financed the atomic projects, the scientists without whom atomic energy would still be locked in mystery, the free enterprisers who built and operated the atomic plants and the whole complex of American free enterprise. . . .

Present Policy

What is the present policy?

First. The United States Government is sole owner of all fissionable material and production facilities. It also exercises complete control over all fissionable materials.

Second. The government controls all uses of fissionable materials.

Third. The government's primary objective is the production and use of atomic energy for national defense.

Fourth. The government's secondary objective is the development of peacetime benefits as excess fissionable materials over defense requirements become available.

Advocating Changes in Policy

What changes are advocated in formulating future policy?

First. The government would relinquish its sole ownership and control of fissionable material and production facilities to private enterprise. Relinquishment of sole government ownership must of necessity weaken security controls.

Second. The government will relinquish to private enterprise the peacetime benefits of atomic energy—civilian power, industrial uses, biological and medicinal, and so forth.

The primary use of all atomic energy for defense is not changed under proposals made to date.

Third. The government would cease to be the sole producer of fissionable material. Private enterprise would become coproducers with the government. Sale or lease of existing plants or subsidized construction of new facilities would appear to be indicated.

We see then that these proposals embody a complete change in our national policy. Let there be no mistake or confusion on this conclusion.

Let us consider some of the reasons for the present policy and also some of the dangers of changing these policies.

First. Government was given a monopoly on the ownership, production, and control of atomic energy by an almost unanimous action of the Congress of the United States in 1946—the Atomic Energy Act of 1946.

This policy was adopted after nine months of hearings and consideration on the subject. It was not adopted capriciously or without extensive debate and intensive consideration of all known factors. Among those primary factors were:

(a) The technological ability to split the atom gave to mankind a basic new source of energy, the effect of which could not be foreseen in our society, economy, or world relationship by Congress.

(b) The possession of this new source of energy and its use as a weapon of destruction held potentialities so powerful and so terrible that only government could be trusted with its use and control.

(c) The development of the use of atomic energy for defense was a primary responsibility for self-preservation of our own and other free world governments.

(d) The development and storage of atomic weapons and the decision as to when they should be used was a necessary and sole responsibility of government.

(e) The tremendously important factor of security, the guarding of the secrets of production of uranium 235 and plutonium, the mechanical gadgetry of atomic bombs and weapons, the storage and control of weapons, and so forth.

(f) The scarcity of fissionable raw material made sole government ownership necessary both from the standpoint of defense needs, accountability of the over-all supply, and danger of possible diversion.

(g) Provision was made for research and development for peacetime uses. The Atomic Energy Commission was authorized and directed to promote peacetime uses through contracts and financial grants to private industry and private laboratories.

(h) In the declaration of policy, section 1 of the Atomic Energy Act of 1946, the paramount objective was "assuring the common defense and security" and four additional but secondary objectives followed: First, "improving the public welfare"; second, "increasing the standard of living"; third, "strengthening free competition in private enterprise"; and fourth, "promoting world peace."

Problems We Face

In the propaganda for basic legislative changes in the act, no arguments are made as to changed conditions which would seriously impair the original justification of the principles outlined in (a), (b), (c), and (d). Let us consider paragraphs (e), (f), (g), and (h) separately.

Paragraph (e), security: Certainly the problem of security would have to be reexamined thoroughly before policy changes that would widen the base of participation by changing the custody and control of atomic energy in quantities sufficient to construct bombs or weapons. Would American corporations with foreign affiliates be eligible? Would the government be responsible for the security procedures and atomic materials after ownership of same was transferred to private hands? Many questions are suggested on this problem, not the least of which is the spreading of police clearance of individuals to a great segment of private industry heretofore free from such restriction.

Paragraph (f): Have fissionable materials become so abundant that substantial quantities necessary for industrial power use can be diverted from the primary purpose—defense of the nation? Has the full development of military uses in the tactical as well as strategic field been achieved?

Unless an affirmative answer can be given to the two preceding questions then the whole propaganda structure for immediate or near future civilian atomic power use is moot. I state without fear of contradiction that the answer is "No." Fissionable material continues to be extremely scarce and costly. The military use has not been scratched. Our supply of atomic weapons, while considerable in some forms, is dangerously inadequate both as to quantity and variety. The President and the Chiefs of Staff are duty bound to testify on this point before Congress can legislate wisely.

The President must advise the Joint Committee on Atomic Energy the effect which present diversion of raw material from mutual defense objectives to corporate-owned civilian power projects would have on our foreign relations.

The problem of wide industrial use and its attendant danger of diversion either as to fissionable material or "know-how" into enemy hands is a problem of immense complexity.

Paragraph (g): A careful analysis of the Atomic Energy Commission's program of encouraging research and development of atomic energy for peacetime purposes will persuade, in my opinion, the most doubtful that they have been vigorous advocates for such development. . . .

Private Industry Wary of Capital Risk

The only tangible suggestion from private industry to date has been that of being willing to start spending a small amount of money on reactor development. Such activity on their part is contingent however, on continued heavy Federal investment in research and development. The pooling of present knowledge and the pooling of any progress made during the so-called interim period is requested. When this interim period has passed—possibly three to five years—the assumption is that private industry will proceed under its own financing. But, in the background of this interim period cooperation lies the real threat to the public interest, that is, the acquisition of patent advantages for special interests.

These advantages cannot be granted on any basis of merit, nor can they be granted without doing violence to the objectives of Congress as set forth in the Atomic Energy Act of 1946, as amended. It is obvious that drastic changes in the basic act would be necessary before such patents could be granted. Drastic legislation would dynamite the present program.

Disruption of Present Program Dangerous

Any disturbance in the present program would cause unpredictable delay and dissolution of the efficient team of technicians now engaged in the effort. No one can predict the time period which would intervene before basic legislative changes would be passed by Congress. Certainly such changes would be fraught with deep controversy. They involve basic ideological concepts of government versus private ownership in the power field, fears of security risks, difference of opinion as to timing and other important factors.

No adequate offer to take over research and development of atomic reactors for civilian power has been made by responsible free enterprise on a private capital risk basis.

The foregoing statement may come as a great surprise to the people who have been absorbing the propaganda articles inspired by interviews and speeches of industrialists, some of the Atomic Energy Commissioners—past and present— and others. Articles frequently are slanted by special article writers to convey a point of view not justified by the full context of the speech or interview. On the other hand, speeches and interview statements sometimes are slanted to promote a specific viewpoint. . . .

Behind all the propaganda and agitation lies the desire to take over the people's $12 billion investment for selfish, and I fear, monopolistic benefit. Behind all the tentative proposals on the part of those who would now take over peacetime potentialities of atomic energy lies a Federal subsidy "gimmick" of one kind or another.

We invite free enterprise to come forward with a bona fide, private capital risk proposal in the atomic power field. We invite them to make such a proposal based on clearly defined legislative changes in the Atomic Energy Act of 1946, as amended. The taxpayers and their representatives in Congress are entitled to a clarification of the issue. They are entitled to an explanation of the hidden-ball play, which apparently is being used behind the subterfuge of "now is the time for private enterprise to take over the atomic power development program."

[On February 10, 1955, the Consolidated Edison Company of New York announced that it planned to construct an atomic furnace with its own funds. The company stated that it would soon apply for a license from the Atomic Energy Commission under the terms of the Atomic Energy Act of 1954.—Ed.]

Fallacies and Danger

Practically all of the propaganda focalizes on the oft repeated statement "before private enterprise can really do a job in atomic power development there must be basic legislative changes"—there are two fallacies in this statement and behind these fallacies lies a danger.

The first fallacy is the inference or assumption that private enterprise has been shackled, held back, slowed down, and prevented from doing a good job to date. This inferred premise is not true and its untruth is proven: (a) by the phenomenal progress made in this new field during the seven years of the Commission's existence; (b) its untruth is attested by repeated testimony from contractual industrial and management firms who have participated in the program. As a matter of fact, progress has been accelerated by access to almost unlimited tax funds, far beyond the willingness or capacity for development based on private risk capital.

The second fallacy is that there must be basic legislative changes in the Atomic Energy Act of 1946, as amended, in order to guarantee a continuance of progress. I denounce this assumption on at least two counts: There has been no slowup in research and development in the reactor—atomic power for civilian uses—program, and I cite the atomic-powered submarine reactor which is now a reality in proto-type. . . . I cite other publicly known projects such as the development of an aircraft carrier type of atomic marine propulsion engine and a nuclear aircraft engine. While these latter projects are not in as advanced stage as the atomic submarine project, no complaint as to progress has been made by responsible persons.

I maintain that the present possibilities of private enter-prise participation under existing law have not been fully explored nor have those possibilities been exhausted by the Commission. I admit frankly that many difficulties have been presented to the Commission; difficulties which, in the main, they have solved. There is, in my opinion, no insurmount-able obstacle toward continued private enterprise participa-tion. There has been no boycott by private enterprise. The impressive list of great corporations which are now engaged in this program proves my point.

I stated that behind these two fallacies lies a danger, and I believe that I should explain this statement.

That danger is premature or ill-considered legislative changes in the present Atomic Energy Act which might under attractive and oversimplified objectives: (a) interrupt our present rapid rate of research, development, and produc-tion; (b) endanger security and United States primacy in the atomic field by widening the base of security risk; (c) handicap free competitive enterprise and promote private monopoly in future peacetime uses and benefits of atomic energy. In regard to (a), any basic legislative change must be preceded by extensive hearings as this is of major na-tional and international importance. . . .

Security a Real Problem

In regard to (b), widening the base of free enterprise participation on a competitive basis by relinquishing owner-

ship and control of bombmaking quantities of U235 or plutonium or substantially enriched U238 would magnify the task
of maintaining security to a dangerous degree. Until this
one problem is solved, the whole subject is moot.

In regard to (c), I wish to deal with this subject in a
more complete manner by referring to paragraph (h) and
the four principles appurtenant thereto.

As I pointed out in the aforementioned paragraph (h),
the declaration of policy in section 1 of the Atomic Energy
Act stated that the paramount objective was "assuring the
common defense and security" and the four secondary, but
correlative objectives were: first, "improving the public
welfare"; second, "increasing the standard of living"; third,
"strengthening free competition in private enterprise";
fourth, "promoting world peace."

It is evident that three of these four objectives, one, two,
and four, are end objectives in the nature of national and
international improvement in the well-being and safety of
the individual; it is also evident that objective three is specific as to the method to be used to attain the other three end
objectives and it is to objective three that I wish to address
my remarks.

Question of Free Competition

The capitalistic system, as developed in the United States,
modified and regulated by state and Federal laws in the interest of our society, has produced the greatest good for the
largest number of people compared to any politico-economic
system yet demonstrated in history.

The tendency of our system to develop business of tremendous size and power, the threat of semimonopoly, monopoly, or powerful combinations in restraint of competitive
trade has been recognized by the Federal legislators.

Laws have been passed in the national interest to prevent
concentration of economic power to the extent considered
inimical to the public interest. Due chiefly, in my opinion,
to the effect of this type of regulatory legislation and to a
growth of social responsibility on the part of American busi-

ness leaders, the old "public be damned" attitude has gradually been replaced by a "public be served" philosophy. This new sense of social responsibility was written into the basic purpose of the Atomic Energy Act of 1946, and its subsequent amendments did not change this principle.

Clearly set forth in the first section of the act's declaration of policy were these words, "strengthening free competition." In order to effectuate this policy as well as others, a system of permissive licensing was set up in section 7 of the act. . . .

The Congress could not foresee "the effect of the use of atomic energy for civilian purposes upon the social, economic and political structures" in the future, but it did anticipate that, "tapping this new source of energy will cause profound changes in our present way of life." They therefore wrote into the act, and prescribed administrative directions to safeguard the capitalistic principle of "strengthening free competition." The Congress went beyond this declaration of policy and expressly prohibited licensing for industrial purposes, "where activities under any license might serve to maintain or foster the growth of monopoly, restraint of trade, unlawful competition or other trade position inimical to the entry of new, freely competitive enterprises in the field." . . .

I believe that these principles are basic to the perpetuation of our democracy. I believe the Congress was more than usually aware of the fact that they were dealing with a subject matter fraught with tremendous significance for the future. Selfishness, greed, partisanship and personal bitterness was laid aside in the presence of this new discovery of almost unlimited energy.

The sole objective of the people's representatives was to enact legislation in the interest of all the people.

No Improvement in Peace Prospects

The compelling realities that existed in 1946 are still with us today. In fact, world conditions have deteriorated rather than improved.

Military needs have not, nor will they in the near future, be fulfilled.

Our conventional sources of civilian power—coal, oil, hydroelectric—are adequate for the foreseeable future.

No immediate emergency faces us that would justify substantial diversion of raw uranium material into civilian power use.

No real justification can be given for widening the security risk which is indivisible from relinquishment of government ownership and control.

The public interest will not be served at this time by trading off the people's $12 billion investment to date, for a few million dollars of private risk capital.

INDUSTRY BIDS FOR ATOMIC POWER [6]

Probably the most significant single economic decision of our time is under consideration by the Congress of the United States. On this decision will hinge the very future of industrial enterprise and the progress of the one universal which stands as essential to modern living and efficiency—power.

The decision of the Congress will be twofold. It will determine (1) if the secret of atomic energy can be released to carefully selected industrialists for the generating of electrical power; and (2) whether our government will follow a path of many years' standing and subsidize application of the atom to so-called private purposes, or will require prospective users and beneficiaries to finance their own experiments and operations.

The way Congress decides these matters will have a tremendous impact on business. And we will doubtless hear plenty about it as the legislators make up their minds. There is misunderstanding both about the aims and desires of in-

[6] From article by James W. Irwin, counselor of chemical, pharmaceutical, and other companies on public, stockholder, and employee relations. *Harvard Business Review*. 31:36-50. July-August 1953. Reprinted by permission. (Mr. Irwin's article was written prior to the revision of the Atomic Energy Act.)

dustrialists with regard to atomic energy and about the needs of the people for more and possibly cheaper power in localities where fuels are now desperately short or not available at all. From these misunderstandings there will develop conflicts about private development of atomic power—not lukewarm disagreements of minor principles and policies, but bitter, vitriolic, and, in some instances, viciously and maliciously inspired campaigns designed to discredit industry as a whole, the political administration which sponsors any enabling legislation, and all the men who spearhead the thinking.

In this article I want to discuss the highly controversial questions surrounding the application of atomic energy to commercial use and also the vital matter of ownership and control of atomic power plants. . . .

Private Ownership?

From now on until the installation of the first . . . [private] facilities begins to become a fact, there is a long and rocky road involving complicated legislation, the formation of a new attitude toward industrial patent application, a liberalizing of feeling about the divulging of information relating to the atom, and a faith on the part of investors to a degree probably never previously registered.

Throughout all these discussions the strong feelings and attitudes that different parties have about the highly "loaded" question of private versus public ownership will be of great influence. In addition to the preconceived emotional biases that always enter into a question of this sort, opinions will vary according to the weight attached to certain key arguments.

The Pros

Some of the outstanding arguments in favor of private control are these:

(1) The development of a new method of generating electric power using atomic energy will be costly. Estimates for a 200,000 kilowatt plant range in the vicinity of $25 mil-

lion, exclusive of the section of the plant properly chargeable to production of the by-product plutonium. Since there will be many generating plants following the early ones, the burden upon taxpayers will be extremely high unless private companies rather than government agencies are permitted to carry on the work and do their own financing.

(2) The technical problems to be solved before power can be economically and competitively generated by this method are tremendous. The granting of permission to private industry will in itself insure devotion to the task of the extraordinary ingenuity of engineers and scientists from every branch of industry—particularly chemical, utility, and electrical equipment manufacturing. The age-long rivalry between the companies making up these industries will accelerate development. The know-how that has come about through cooperation of utility operators with engineers of equipment manufacturers, and that has brought the cost of electricity almost steadily downward, will again work in behalf of the public and reduce the cost of application of this new power source.

(3) Private capital for generating plants will not add to the great amount of national debt already represented in government-owned power systems. Today the Federal Government owns more than one tenth of the nation's power capacity, representing a sizable share of the national debt. This investment should not be increased when the same result, probably more efficiently administered, can be accomplished with private capital and absolutely no additional investment by the taxpayer.

(4) The income resulting from such new power facilities will result in payment of income taxes to the Federal and state governments involved, and property and franchise taxes to the local governments, still further reducing the burden upon taxpayers. Federally owned power facilities not only increase the national debt and the interest burden of the taxpayers, but never pay any income taxes, seldom pay state and local taxes, and thus result in doubly increased cost to the taxpayer.

The Cons

Offsetting the pros are a few generally recognized cons:

(1) The cost of development of power using atomic energy may be so great that private business cannot or will not finance such an operation to the extent necessary to capitalize fully on the technical developments available as rapidly as now is possible. If this should turn out to be the case, there could be little valid objection to the granting of development contracts by the government to expedite the work, as is now done in almost every phase of military equipment experimental work.

(2) With the cost high, one or two large companies might be the only ones to enter the field seriously, and they might attain such development that a situation leaning toward monopoly could come about. However, we already have suitable safeguards in use with other facilities, so it should not be too difficult with properly written legislation to avoid abuses in this direction.

(3) The development of electric power phases of atomic energy might disclose valuable information to enemy agents. Adequate safeguards must be provided against this possibility, but we have military precedents to help us here, too. All employees working on secret government contracts supposedly are carefully screened. . . .

Conclusion

Here are the conclusions that stand out on the basis of the evidence at this time:

The future power needs of the nation—a doubling within the next decade—require development of electric generating facilities from sources other than coal and oil.

The production of such power in dual-reactor plants poses a serious by-product problem. What should be done with the huge quantities of plutonium in the event that the government's stockpile of atomic weapons reaches a level beyond which it would be unwise and uneconomic for it to go?

Industry never has let the problem of an unusable by-product bother it for long or stymie its plans. It is a reasonable assumption that the ingenuity of our physicists, chemists, and engineers will bring about some use for plutonium other than strictly war purposes—possibly as an additional heat source for further power generation. . . .

Protection of the atomic secret is important, but the chemical industry is accustomed to keeping secrets. Besides, there is every reason to believe that most of the vital specifications are already known to our enemies.

The licensing of a few companies to use the atom must be handled in such a way that those companies are not given a competitive advantage in the making of their products that will serve to promote monopoly by driving out of the market producers of similar products who are not enjoying the benefits of atomic power. . . .

Unused resources in remote areas of the nation (and the world) will be brought into use because power generating facilities can be taken to them, complete with fuel. . . .

The handicaps to industry ownership and operation are many, but the incentive of accomplishment plus the incentive of a reasonable profit return, even though limited and much lower than the chemical industry likes, will cause the program to move rather rapidly, once the wraps of restrictive laws are removed. . . .

The atomic power development should be financed privately without burden on the taxpayers other than accelerated amortization. . . .

Investors need have no fears about the values of holdings in utility companies generating power by conventional means, nor in companies which manufacture utility equipment. Investments in petroleum companies should not be affected in a rising economy, but investments in the coal industry, which is on the downgrade anyway, should be scrutinized carefully. Investments in railroads also may be affected adversely.

Investors should not put money into companies whose sole purpose is the promotion of atomic power generating plants, but they should have no qualms whatsoever about investing in utilities and chemical companies where the atomic project will be just one egg in the basket.

An open-minded student of government versus private sponsorship, financing, and operation of any phase of industry cannot say flatly that there should be no government in business.

Our railroad, highway, and air transportation systems all moved forward more rapidly with government land grants and federally supported highways and air lanes; and, insofar as plane and engine design is concerned, the military financed a sizable share of engineering costs. Nor can anyone overlook the fact that great power projects such as the Hoover Dam would never have been built by private utilities, simply because the uncertainty of power use and sale and a return on investment made the application of private funds extremely risky.

But the government, in behalf of the people, has already financed the basic atomic program as a military measure. The time now seems appropriate and the climate of public thinking just about right to entrust future development to the type of mind which has always contributed more to the public welfare than bureaucracy ever has or ever can.

BIBLIOGRAPHY

An asterisk (*) preceding a reference indicates that the article or a part of it has been reprinted in this book.

BOOKS, PAMPHLETS, AND DOCUMENTS

Association for Supervision and Curriculum Development. Large was our bounty: natural resources and the schools: 1948 yearbook. 216p. The Association. National Education Association. 1201 16th St. Washington 6, D.C. '48.

Carhart, A. H. Timber in your life. 317p. J. B. Lippincott Co. Philadelphia. '55.

Carskadon, T. R. and Modley, Rudolf. U.S.A.: The measure of a nation. 101p. Macmillan Co. New York. '49.

Chamber of Commerce of the United States. Natural Resources Department. Policy declarations on natural resources, 1954. 41p. The Chamber. 1615 H St. Washington 6, D.C. '54.

Chase National Bank of the City of New York. Peacetime prospects of atomic energy. 31p. The Bank. 11 Broad St. New York 15. '54.

Dewhurst, J. F. and others. America's needs and resources. 812p. Twentieth Century Fund. New York. '47.

Funk, Ollie. Conservation for tomorrow's America. 144p. Ohio Division of Conservation and Natural Resources. Columbus. '42.

Furnas, S. V. M. and Furnas, Clifford. Man, bread, and destiny. 364p. Garden City Publishing Co. Garden City, N.Y. '42.

Greene, L. S. and others. Rescued earth; a study of natural resources in Tennessee. 204p. University of Tennessee Press. Knoxville. '48.

Hatcher, Helene. Better living through wise use of resources. 76p. United States Office of Education. Supt. of Docs. Washington 25, D.C. '50.

Izaak Walton League of America. Education in conservation of our natural resources. 32p. The League. 31 N. State St. Chicago 2. '44.

Lapp, R. E. The new force: the story of atoms and people. 238p. Harper and Bros. New York. '53.

National Association of Manufacturers. Industrial future of atomic energy. 33p. The Association. 2 E. 48th St. New York 17. '54.

National Industrial Conference Board. Mobilizing for atomic war. 66p. The Board. 247 Park Ave. New York 17. '50.

*National Industrial Conference Board. Resources: from abundance to scarcity by 1975? (Studies in Business Economics no36) 52p. The Board. 247 Park Ave. New York 17. '52.

Newman, J. R. and Miller, B. S. Control of atomic energy; a study of its social, economic, and political implications. 434p. McGraw-Hill Book Co. New York. '48.

*Resources for the Future, Inc. Nation looks at its resources; report of the Mid-Century Conference on Resources for the Future, Washington, D.C., December 2, 3, 4, 1953. 418p. Resources for the Future, Inc. 1145 19th St. N.W. Washington, D.C. '54.
    Reprinted in this book: Public lands—who should control them? R. W. Sawyer; W. A. D'Ewart. p361-5.

*Stead, W. H. Economic problems of natural resources. 69p. mimeo. Joint Council on Economic Education. 2 W. 46th St. New York 36. '55.

Straus, M. W. Why not survive? 272p. Simon & Schuster. New York. '55.

United States. Congress. Joint Committee on Atomic Energy. Atomic energy; summary of the hearing on atomic power development and private enterprise. 23p. 83d Congress, 1st session. Supt. of Docs. Washington 25, D.C. '53.

United States. Department of Agriculture. Our forest resources: what they are and what they mean to us. 37p. Supt. of Docs. Washington 25, D.C. '54.

United States. Department of the Interior. Annual report of the Secretary of the Interior, fiscal year ended June 30, 1952. 502p. Supt. of Docs. Washington 25, D.C. '52.

United States. Department of the Interior. National resources and foreign aid; report of J. A. Krug, Secretary of the Interior. 97p. The Department. Washington 25, D.C. '47.

United States. Department of State. Energy resources of the world. 2d ed. 128p. Supt. of Docs. Washington 25, D.C. '49.

United States. National Security Resources Board. Objectives of United States materials resources policy and suggested initial steps in their accomplishment. 101p. Supt. of Docs. Washington 25, D.C. '52.

United States. National Security Resources Board. Report to the President by the chairman (of the National Security Resources Board). 40p. The Board. Washington, D.C. '53.

*United States. President's Materials Policy Commission [Paley Commission]. Resources for freedom; a report to the President. 5v. Supt. of Docs. Washington 25, D.C. '52.

United States. President's Water Resources Policy Commission. Report. 3v. Supt. of Docs. Washington 25, D.C. '50-'51.

Woytinsky, W. S. and Woytinsky, E. S. World population and production. 1268p. Twentieth Century Fund. New York. '53.

*Zimmermann, E. W. World resources and industries. 832p. Harper and Brothers. New York. '51.

PERIODICALS

America. 89:106-7. Ap. 25, '53. Federal lands: a national heritage. E. J. Poulsen.

America. 89:125-6. My. 2, '53. Oil to the coastal states.

America. 89:269-71. Je. 6, '53. Public lands and private enterprise. R. L. Schueler.

America. 89:350. Jl. 4, '53. Creeping socialism.

America. 91:349. Jl. 3, '54. White House slap at TVA.

America. 91:530. S. 27, '54. Mitchell's charges; Dixon-Yates power plant.

American Forests. 59:14+. F. '53. Traditional GOP land policies. G. H. Collingwood.

*American Forests. 59:15+. F. '53. Way back to land freedom. L. F. Lee.

American Forests. 59:8-9+. Mr. '53. Profiteering with impunity. Cleveland van Dresser.

American Forests. 59:10-12+. Ap. '53. They still covet our lands. A. H. Carhart.

American Forests. 59:18-19+. Je. '53. Emotionalism on the public range; square deal for half a century. D. A. Fulton and C. M. Granger.

American Forests. 59:28. O. '53. McKay denies give away charges.

American Forests. 59:20-2+. N. '53. Is this creeping socialism? W. M. Baker.

American Forests. 60:10-13+. Ja. '54. Look at the future of resources.

American Forests. 60:31. Jl. '54. What about the Hope-Aiken grazing bills?

American Forests. 60:32-3. Jl. '54. Pattern for grazing legislation.

American Forests. 60:34-6. Jl. '54. In defense of the Aiken Grazing Bill. H. B. Woodward.

American Forests. 60:36+. Jl. '54. In opposition to the proposed legislation (the Aiken Grazing Bill).

American Forests. 60:2. S. '54. Reply (on the Hope-Aiken grazing bills). H. B. Woodward.

American Mercury. 74:97-8. My. '52. Mr. Daniel on the tidelands oil case decision; television program.

American Mercury. 75:96-9. Jl. '52. Secretary Chapman on the tidelands issue and Federal power; television program.

*Annals of the American Academy of Political and Social Science. 281:1-202. My. '52. Future of our natural resources; ed. by Stephen Raushenbush [entire issue].
      Reprinted in this book: Private forestry in transition. S. T. Dana. p84-92.

Annals of the American Academy of Political and Social Science. 290:1-6. N. '53. Atomic energy and the democratic process. R. A. Dahl.

Annals of the American Academy of Political and Social Science. 290:35-44. N. '53. Economic technology of nuclear power. J. A. Lane.

Annals of the American Academy of Political and Social Science. 290:62-6. N. '53. Some economic consequences of nuclear power. Walter Isard and R. A. Kavesh.

Annals of the American Academy of Political and Social Science. 290:76-81. N. '53. Congress and the atom. H. M. Jackson.

Atlantic Monthly. 189:29-32. Je. '52. Our inexhaustible resources. Eugene Holman.

    Same abridged. Reader's Digest. 61:93-6. Jl. '52; *Reply.* Atlantic Monthly. 190:29. O. '52. D. J. Zinn.

*Baltimore. 46:11+. My. '53. Tidelands: a basic national issue. Hall Hammond.

Barron's. p 1. Ag. 30, '54. Atomic diversion.

*Bulletin of the Atomic Scientists. 9:109-44. My. '53. Atomic energy and private enterprise—symposium; Part I.

    Reprinted in this book: Should we break our biggest monopoly? A. P. Lerner. p 110-14+.

Bulletin of the Atomic Scientists. 9:135-40+, 309-14, 341-4, 380-2. My., O., N., D. '53. Atomic power and private enterprise; summary of the [congressional] Joint Committee report.

Bulletin of the Atomic Scientists. 9:156-75. Je. '53. Atomic energy and private enterprise—symposium; Part II.

Bulletin of the Atomic Scientists. 9:305-8. O. '53. Atomic power as a risk venture. Karl Cohen.

Bulletin of the Atomic Scientists. 9:314. O. '53. Nuclear power development; AEC policy statement. Gordon Dean.

Bulletin of the Atomic Scientists. 9:348. N. '53. Current comment; great debate; quotations from various leaders.

Bulletin of the Atomic Scientists. 10:100-2. Mr. '54. Franchise for atomic energy.

Business Week. p26. Mr. 17, '51. U.S. shifts stockpile policy.

Business Week. p26. N. 24, '51. Stockpilers have a new approach.

Business Week. p 136. Je. 21, '52. Empty oil leases.

Business Week. p33. Ag. 30, '52. U.S. stockpile; now a price prop.

Business Week. p92-4. F. 14, '53. Who will get Northwest's power in harness?

Business Week. p32. Mr. 14, '53. Coming up: an atomic policy.

Business Week. p29. My. 2, '53. Industry's hopes for atom rise.

Business Week. p32. Je. 13, '53. Power contracts.

*Business Week. p77-8. Je. 27, '53. Tidelands oil won't produce any fortunes overnight.

Business Week. p34. Jl. 18, '53. Hydropower: government backs out.

Business Week. p32. Ag. 8, '53. Atomic change to give private industry bigger role.

Business Week. p34. Ag. 22, '53. Administration codifies new power policy.

Business Week. p36. Ag. 22, '53. Priority for the atom.

Business Week. p63-4+. S. 12, '53. McKay: changing a power trend.

Business Week. p 130. O. 10, '53. Dams, cables, Congress.

Business Week. p 120+. O. 24, '53. Atomic forum for peaceful atom uses.

Business Week. p32. N. 28, '53. Hydrogamble.

Business Week. p 126+. D. 12, '53. Resources: the plot thickens.

Business Week. p 180+. D. 12, '53. Next great frontier.

Business Week. p30. D. 19, '53. Private power will play bigger role in Northwest.

Business Week. p29. F. 13, '54. Fight over TVA's future.

Business Week. p28. F. 27, '54. New fight on public power.

Business Week. p30. F. 27, '54. Private atom.

Business Week. p28. Ap. 24, '54. Toward private atom plants.

Business Week. p32. Jl. 24, '54. Embattled TVA.

Business Week. p27. Ag. 7, '54. TVA and Fed get Eisenhower men.

Business Week. p27. Ag. 21, '54. Atom goes private.

Business Week. p34. Ag. 28, '54. Self-help tempered with mercy.

Business Week. p31-2. S. 11, '54. Power deal ready for signing.

Business Week. p 188-94. O. 16, '54. Changing AEC in midstream.

Christian Century. 69:1020. S. 10, '52. Oil enters the campaign.

Christian Century. 70:468. Ap. 22, '53. Offshore oil and the public domain.

Christian Century. 70:535-6. My. 6, '53. Conservation no party issue.
    Reply. 70:633. My. 27, '53. James Stevens.

Christian Century. 70:595. My. 20, '53. Offshore oil vote warns conservationists.

Collier's. 129:70. Mr. 8, '52. On the brink of socialism.

Collier's. 131:34-5+. Ja. 10, '53. What's left in Uncle Sam's pantry? J. D. Ratcliff.

Collier's. 131:70-6. Je. 20, '53. Scandal of the Paducah atom project. J. F. Dinneen.

Commercial and Financial Chronicle. 177:2201+. My. 21, '53. Public power is here to stay. Douglas McKay.

Commercial and Financial Chronicle. 178:2267. D. 10, '53. Impact of atomic energy on the industrial economy. Walter Isard.

Commercial and Financial Chronicle. 178:2636+. D. 31, '53. Industrial atomic energy. J. J. Grebe.

Commercial and Financial Chronicle. 178:2636-7+. D. 31, '53. Industry should have greater share in nuclear development. E. M. Zuckert.

Commonweal. 56:188. My. 30, '52. Oil's role in the campaign.

Commonweal. 58:88. My. 1, '53. Raids on the public domain.

Commonweal. 58:194. My. 28, '53. Fight for TVA.

Commonweal. 58:218. Je. 5, '53. Threat to conservation.

Commonweal. 58:312. Jl. 3, '53. Gibe at the TVA.

Commonweal. 58:529-30. S. 4, '53. New power policy.

*Congressional Digest. 32:289-314. D. '53. Problem of the public lands; background material and pro and con discussion of the D'Ewart uniform grazing bill [entire issue].

    Reprinted in this book: Differing views on final disposition. P. W. Rodino, Jr.; L. C. Hunt. p296-7+.

Fortune. 45:110-17+. F. '52. Triumph of the empire builders.

Fortune. 46:114-17+. Ag. '52. Crisis in raw materials; condensed from report by the President's Materials Policy Commission.

Fortune. 47:142-7+. Je.; 48:105-9+. Jl. '53. The atom: ready for business? Eric Hodgins.

Fortune. 48:127-8. O. '53. McKay gets mired in the middle of the road.

*Guaranty Survey (Guaranty Trust Company). 34:1-3. N. '54. Give away what?

Harper's Magazine. 204:6+. Mr. '52. Bonanza for education. Lister Hill.

Harper's Magazine. 205:65-8. O. '52. Old steal refurbished. Bernard De Voto.

Harper's Magazine. 206:53-6. F. '53. Billion dollar jackpot. Bernard De Voto.

Harper's Magazine. 206:57-60. My. '53. Sturdy corporate home-steader. Bernard De Voto.

Harper's Magazine. 207:49-52. Jl. '53. Heading for the last round-up. Bernard De Voto.

    Reply, with rejoinder. 207:20-2. O. '53. R. L. Bowditch.

Harper's Magazine. 209:66-74. Ag. '54. Conservation: down and on the way out. Bernard De Voto.

*Harvard Business Review. 31:36-50. Jl.-Ag. '53. Industry bids for atomic power. J. W. Irwin.

Harvard Law Review. 66:1450-96. Je. '53. Atomic Energy Act and the private production of atomic power. O. M. Ruebhausen and R. B. von Mehren.

Journal of Business of the University of Chicago. 27:312-20. O. '54. Industrial application of atomic energy. H. D. Smyth.

Land and Land News. 12:87-91+. Spring '53. Conservation tangle: a symposium of opinion with editorial comment.

Life. 35:27-31. N. 9, '53. Issue: U.S. or private dams.

    Discussion. 35:4+. N. 30, '53.

Magazine of Wall Street. 93:606-7+. F. 20, '54. Liquidating government's $30 billion business empire. H. DuBois.

Monthly Letter on Economic Conditions and Government Finance (National City Bank of New York). p45-7. Ap. '54. Public vs. private power at Niagara.

Nation. 173:183. S. 8, '51. Is California part of the union?

Nation. 176:197. Mr. 7, '53. Sauce for the shrimp.

Nation. 176:317. Ap. 18, '53. Year of decision.

Nation. 176:407-8. My. 16, '53. Tidelands oil and the political tides.

Nation. 176:416-17. My. 16, '53. Give it away! Ike's great crusade. N. W. Strauss.

Nation. 176:466+. Je. 6, '53. Grab for the atom. Leland Olds.

Nation. 176:531-3. Je. 20, '53. Threat to all TVA's. Bruce Catton.

Nation. 178:48. Ja. 16, '54. Here's the score on the GOP's giveaway. Harry Levine.

Nation. 179:30-2. Jl. 10, '54. Great atomic giveaway. Leland Olds.

Nation. 179:50-3. Jl. 17, '54. People's atom. Leland Olds.

Nation. 179:84. Jl. 31, '54. Containing the TVA.

*Nation. 179:269-96. O. 2, '54. Great giveaway [entire issue].
    Reprinted in this book: Great giveaway. p269-72; Whose atom is it? p278-9; Oil under the sea. p280.

Nation's Business. 42:48-50. Ja. '54. Resources return to the people. Douglas McKay.

Nature Magazine. 46:90-2+. F. '53. Forest land steal. Cleveland van Dresser.

New Republic. 124:17. Mr. 26, '51. Oil befouls our political life. H. L. Ickes.

New Republic. 124:17. Ap. 2, '51. Bright-yellow journalism. H. L. Ickes.

New Republic. 124:13. Ap. 30, '51. New land grab.

New Republic. 125:17. Ag. 20, '51. Gobble-uns'll get you! H. L. Ickes.

New Republic. 125:17. Ag. 27, '51. Big steal in oil. H. L. Ickes.

New Republic. 125:17. S. 10, '51. Smelly oil mendacity. H. L. Ickes.

New Republic. 125:9-10. D. 10, '51. Paging J. Howard McGrath. H. L. Ickes.

New Republic. 126:8. F. 4, '52. Tidelands compromise.

New Republic. 126:7. Ap. 14, '52. Wanted: a presidential veto of quit-claim bill.

New Republic. 128:12-13. Mr. 2, '53. Oil rush of '53. Lister Hill.

New Republic. 128:10-11. Mr. 30, '53. Season for plunder. R. L. Neuberger.

New Republic. 128:7. Ap. 13, '53. Off-shore oil bill; a trillion-dollar principle.

New Republic. 128:5-6. My. 11, '53. Coming struggle for atomic power.

New Republic. 128:4. My. 18, '53. Give-away begins; Senate vote.

New Republic. 128:4. Jl. 20, '53. Wait till after election; Capehart bill.

New Republic. 129:9-11. S. 14, '53. Look out, neighbor; President Eisenhower's new policy. Leland Olds.

New Republic. 129:5. O. 12, '53. Tidelands test.

New Republic. 129:5. D. 7, '53. Twenty long years.

New Republic. 130:3. Ja. 4, '54. End of Bonneville.

New Republic. 130:9-10. Ja. 11, '54. Eisenhower's real decision.

New Republic. 130:4. F. 22, '54. Relieving TVA.

New Republic. 130:4. My. 3, '54. While you weren't looking; give-away number two.

New Republic. 130:5. My. 17, '54. Undermining public power: Pacific Northwest.

New Republic. 130:9. My. 24, '54. Will private monopoly take over our atomic program? Tom Fitzsimmons.

New Republic. 130:2-3. Je. 7, '54. Will we move forward or backward in our development of atomic power?

New Republic. 131:14-16. Jl. 19, '54. Perversion of power; AEC at Paducah, Ky.

New Republic. 131:3. S. 13, '54. Hear no evil, see no evil, speak no evil; Dixon-Yates deal.

New Republic. 131:4. S. 27, '54. High tension; Dixon-Yates power plant.

New Republic. 131:6-11. O. 18, '54. More light on Dixon-Yates. Michael Straight.

*New York Herald Tribune. p 1+. O. 16, '54. Dixon-Yates: the Democratic party's view. Estes Kefauver.

*New York Herald Tribune. p 1+. O. 22, '54. Gains in resources control. Douglas McKay.

*New York Herald Tribune. p 19. N. 11, '54. President on "Dixon-Yates."

New York Times Magazine. p 13+. S. 6, '53. Wide open debate on the wide open spaces. R. L. Neuberger.

Newsweek. 40:108. S. 15, '52. Tidelands issue. Raymond Moley.

Newsweek. 40:86+. O. 27, '52. Private plans.

Newsweek. 41:73. Ja. 19, '53. Tidelands maneuvers.

Newsweek. 41:88-90. Ap. 13, '53. Industry's progress toward harnessing the atom.

Newsweek. 41:112. My. 11, '53. Take, but don't grab. Raymond Moley.

Newsweek. 43:60-2. Mr. 1, '54. Shift to free enterprise.

Newsweek. 43:84+. My. 17, '54. Irrigation, hydropower's expensive partner. Raymond Moley.

Newsweek. 44:16-17. Ag. 2, '54. Talk-talk; issue in the Senate's filibuster on public power.

Newsweek. 44:69. Ag. 9, '54. Working atom: costly; how the government monopoly in atomic energy is being ended.

Quarterly Journal of Economics. 66:327-41. Ag. '52. Raw materials, rearmament and economic development. E. S. Mason.

*Reader's Digest. 63:41-6. Jl. '53. Trust Uncle Sam to get you a power shortage. William Hard and Charles Stevenson.

*Reader's Digest. 64:68-72. Mr. '54. How to get atomic power fastest. William Hard.

*Reporter. 7:25-7. N. 11, '52. Who owns the oil under the sea? Alan Barth.

*Reporter. 8:25-9. My. 12, '53. One-fourth of a nation—public lands and itching fingers. Wallace Stegner.

*Reporter. 9:28-32. D. 8, '53. Don't let TVA be wrecked, Mr. President! F. G. Clement.

*Reporter. 10:23-7. My. 11, '54. Battle for Hells Canyon. Joe Miller.

Reporter. 11:15-16. O. 21, '54. ABC of Dixon-Yates, or how to get less for more. Douglass Cater.

Reporter. 12:27-30. F. 24, '55. 'Partnership' vs, the public interest. R. L. Neuberger.

Review of Economics and Statistics. 36:267-73. Ag. '54. Afterthoughts on Paley. Colin Clark.
        Comment. 36:273-8. Ag. '54. E. S. Mason.

Saturday Evening Post. 225:12. F. 21, '53. Northwest's new big dams prove private power can build 'em. R. O. Case.

Saturday Evening Post. 226:10+. S. 26, '53. Electric power supplied by TVA isn't so cheap. E. A. Stephenson.

Saturday Evening Post. 227:10. Ag. 28, '54. Our free system will put the atom to work.

Science Newsletter. 63:340. My. 30, '53. Competitive atomic power foreseen 15 years hence.

Senior Scholastic. 62:12-13. My. 13, '53. States get tidelands.

Social Science. 28:67-71. Ap. '53. Social trends and atomic energy. J. B. Gittler.

Time. 61:94. Je. 8, '53. Private atomic power.

Time. 62:80. Jl. 20, '53. Private power victory.

Time. 62:7. Ag. 31, '53. Power politics.

Time. 62:95. N. 2, '53. Break for private power.

Time. 62:84. D. 21, '53. Partners' program in the Pacific Northwest.

Time. 63:86-7. Je. 28, '54. Private power wins.

*U.S.A., the Magazine of American Affairs. 1:99-105. Je. '52. Tidelands oil. H. M. Fleming.

*United States Department of State Bulletin. 28:486-7. Mr. 30, '53. Tidelands legislation and the conduct of foreign affairs. J. B. Tate.

United States News & World Report. 32:56-61. My. 9, '52. What's wrong with the atomic energy program; interview. K. S. Pitzer.

*United States News & World Report. 34:25-7. Mr. 27, '53. All public lands going to states?

United States News & World Report. 34:22-4. My. 8, '53. Industry gets set for the atom.

*United States News & World Report. 35:62-6+. O. 9, '53. New policy on electric power; interview. Douglas McKay.

United States News & World Report. 35:49-50. N. 6, '53. New kind of atom race.

United States News & World Report. 37:41-3. Jl. 30, '54. Idea twenty-one years ago, giant today.

*United States News & World Report. 37:27-9. N. 19, '54. ABC's of Dixon-Yates.

United States News & World Report. 37:58-67. D. 17, '54. "We're ahead of Soviets on the H-Bomb"; interview. L. L. Strauss.

*Vital Speeches of the Day. 19:562-6. Jl. 1, '53. Are we ready to give the atom to private enterprise? Melvin Price.

Vital Speeches of the Day. 20:162-5. Ja. 1, '54. Atomic stockpile for peace; text of UN address, December 8, 1953. D. D. Eisenhower.

   Same with title Eisenhower proposes use of atomic stockpile for peace. Commercial and Financial Chronicle. 178:2253+. D. 10, '53; *same with title* Eisenhower's plan for the atom. United States News & World Report. 35:67-70. D. 18, '53.

*Yale Law Journal. 60:1263-1394. D. '51. Atomic energy industry: an experiment in hybridization. J. R. Newman.

United States News & World Report, 25-26-40, X, Q, 22, 6-v-kind of situation.

United States News & World Report, 22, 284, II, 2, U, face twenty-one, three-one-plan, under.

United States News & World Report, 22, 229, N, P, G, Cl., vol. twenty-one.

United States News & World Report, 22, 284, IV, 3, A "Survey Abroad of Soviet" on the H Bomb, interviews, L. Strauss, and Speeches to UN Dec. 16 1953, c., R. 2 "E." free use and private enterprise Atomic Power.

Undersecretary of the Day, 20, 1054, IX, 1954, Atomic stockpile on peace, Text of UN sessions, December 8, 1953, P. D. Eisenhower.

Yale Law Journal, 60, 1260, 1951, Many contracts between Government in private sector.